Communalism EXPLAINED!

-a graphic account

Supported by

Communalism

EXPLAINED!

–a graphic account

Ram Puniyani and Sharad Sharma

VANI PRAKASHAN

VANI PRAKASHAN

4695, 21-A, Daryaganj, New Delhi 110 002
Branch
Ashok Rajpath, Patna 800 204

Phone: +91 11 23273167 Fax: +91 11 23275710
www.vaniprakashan.in
vaniprakashan@gmail.com

Communalism Explained! - a graphic account
by Ram Puniyani and Sharad Sharma

ISBN: 978-93-5000-740-2

Communalism / Comics

First Edition

Acknowledgements
Ink & page making support : Sunder Mohan Murmu

We are thankful to
Neha Buch, Anil Vats, Siddharth Sarathi, Girijesh Kumar, Anil Pandey, Neeraj Khattri, Aparna Khanna, Ashraf Patel, Anurupa Roy, Jaya Battacharji Rose, Julufa Islam Choudhury, Devendra Ojha, Manas Baruah, Tawna, Nida Shams, R.N. Sharma and Rekha Sharma.

Printed at Nice Printing Press, Delhi 110 051

Vani Prakashan's logo is a creation of the strokes from M.F. Husain

About the book

This book is a broad overview of the phenomenon of communalism and terrorism, which has gripped the country and other parts of the World. It takes up the theme in a question-answer format and is enriched by the graphics, which supplement the text. The narrative begins with the demolition of Babri Mosque on 6th December 1992, goes on to the horrific violence, which followed the Babri demolition and tries to understand the forces, which instigate and sustain this violence.

It goes on to the tragedy of Godhra train catching fire and the carnage unleashed on that pretext. It gives the extracts from Citizens Tribunal, Bannerjee Commission and the Tehelka expose on the carnage.

The next chapters take up the understanding of Indian society. The syncretic traditions in the arena of religion, the mixed heritage in the area of literature, art, culture and aspects of social life is outlined. The arrival British lays the foundation of communal politics. The agenda of British colonialists and their manipulation of the landlord sections and landlord-elites' ideology in the communal direction leading to partition tragedy and the sowing the seeds of discord in Kashmir are outlined.

The values emerging form freedom movement, the role of Gandhi in freedom movement, the values of rising classes: Secular democracy in contrast to the communal politics of declining sections of society is compared and contrasted. The book also demolishes the misconceptions about minorities prevalent in the society, like why temples were destroyed, why conversions took place, the truth behind polygamy and more children, the nature of Christian missionary work, the truth behind the politics of terror are outlined in a lucid manner. Finally the book delineates the steps to strengthen secular and democratic values in the society.

This book is an attempt to present the issues at hand in a simple manner for the average reader, students and youth. The question answer form delineates the issues and prompts the reader to think about the topic. The graphic form makes it easy for the reader to comprehend the issues in an easy form.

We wish to thank Nisha Agrawal, K. Kannan (Oxfam India) and Sunder Mohan Murmu (World Comics India) for their valuable support, making it possible to bring out the graphic form of the book. As we aim to increase the awareness about these issues in the society this support will go a long way in helping us achieve our goal.

Ram Puniyani and Sharad Sharma

Foreword

Oxfam India firmly believes in the secular-democratic values enshrined in the Indian Constitution. It believes that secularism is the cornerstone of Indian democracy. It also believes that conflict not only hampers the development process but also adversely affects the poor and the marginalized much more. It is also Oxfam's understanding that communalism is an issue which needs to be made part of general sensitivity of all the development practitioners regardless of their area of work.

Oxfam India would be developing a comprehensive strategy towards this end to make it an integral part of its overall strategy. It would be working towards building partners capacity to develop and promote secular values and to address communal conflict while supporting national advocacy work towards a progressive Communal Violence Bill and revision of National Curriculum framework towards this end.

The book co-authored by Ram Puniyani and Sharad Sharma is a timely publication. It has come out in the market when it was needed the most. The syncretic culture of India and its plural heritage is something we can be proud of but this need to be retold with facts. By supporting this book "Communalism explained - a graphic account" we are simply taking our commitment further.

The book is rich in content and attractive by the look. We hope it will reach the masses and helps them to understand the difference between popular myths and facts prevalent in the Indian society since long.

Nisha Agrawal
CEO, Oxfam India

Content

DEMOLITION OF
BABRI MASJID

It brought to the fore the deep set communalisation of the society and the realization that now communalism is the major problem confronting this society. Though it is such a recent phenomenon it already has been mythified due to the prevalent propaganda.

MYTH

Though the demolition of the Masjid was horrible, we know that it was not a mosque, it was a disputed structure, and you can see Ram Lalla had entered the structure as he (Lord Ram) was deprived of his abode.

FACT

Let's see the sequence of events before we make our judgment:
Dec. 22-23,1949
In 1949 Local district Magistrate reported to state government: few Hindus entered Babri Masjid at the site and installed Ram & Sita idols. (Akhatar, Lucknow, 1997) Government proclaimed the premises as disputed site and locked the gates. The local district magistrate, K.K.Nayyar, a Sangh sympathiser who later became Jan Sangh MP, refused to get the idols removed despite the appeal by the Government, even the appeal of Prime Minister Nehru was ignored. The premises remained locked till 1986.

MYTH

The Hindus were deprived of their place of worship and it was a spontaneous Hindu reaction to take over the place of worship from the pseudo - secular state and the bigoted Muslims.

FACT

Beginning from 1981 there was a heavy communalisation of the social space. Initially in response to the conversion of Dalits in Meenakshipuram the communal forces became very aggressive. Anti-Dalit riots had taken place in Gujarat, more so in Ahmedabad. And since that time they were looking for a provocation to actively spread communal hatred in society.

The incident, which gave boost to the communal politics was signaled by the Shah Bano case. In this the then Govt. of Rajiv Gandhi got the "Muslim women's protection" bill passed by the Parliament to sidetrack the Supreme court's judgment on grant of maintenance to the divorced Muslim women by the Supreme Court. To 'balance' the appeasement of Muslim communal politics, Government played the Hindu communal card and Babri locks were opened at the instance of Hindu Communal forces. In 1985 anti OBC riots took place again in Gujarat.

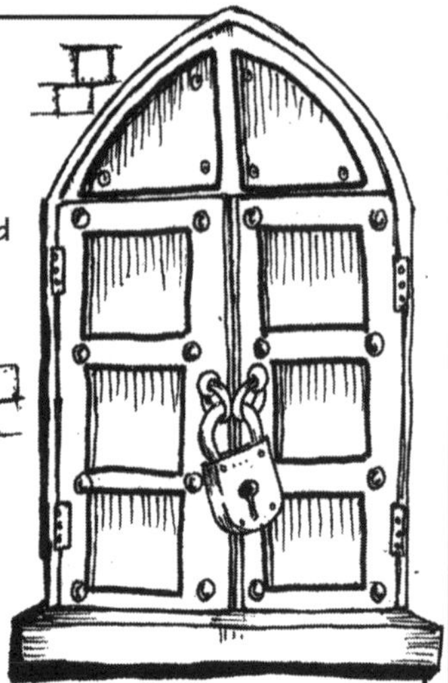

Muslim communal elements supported by the Govt. ensured the scrapping of the Shah Bano judgment.

Mandal commission recommendations were implemented by V P Singh govt. in 1990. In response to this VHP galvanized itself into action on the hysterical cry of 'Save Hinduism', and organized series of campaigns like 'Ekatmata Yagnas' etc. VHP revived the Ayodhya campaign on a higher pitch, resolving to build a magnificent Ram temple at Ayodhya & undertook massive efforts to bring different Hindu religious leaders together on this issue.

6th December, 1992
Kar Sevaks climbing the dome.

Babri mosque flattened. Makeshift temple erected. Idols installed in the makeshift arrangement.

From here BJP took over the Ram Janmbhumi campaign and Advani started his Rath Yatra from Somnath to consolidate the Hindu elite behind the BJP politics.

This led to Kar Seva and Demolition of Mosque-6th December 1992. Babri masjid was declared a disputed structure and the case was pending in the court.

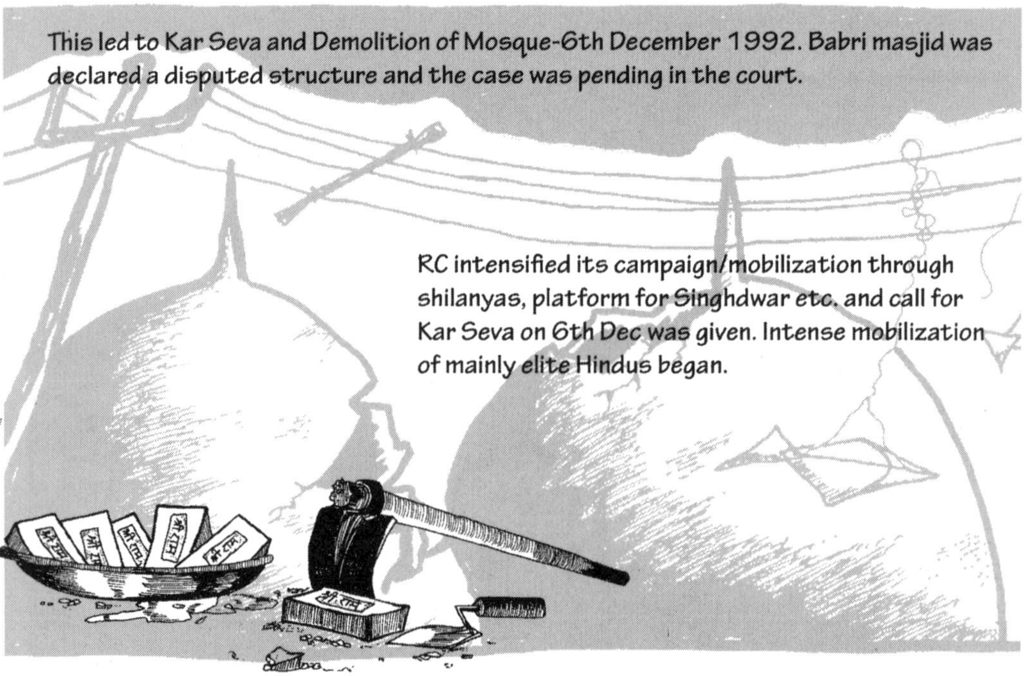

RC intensified its campaign/mobilization through shilanyas, platform for Singhdwar etc. and call for Kar Seva on 6th Dec was given. Intense mobilization of mainly elite Hindus began.

The demolition was a spontaneous act of Hindus whose feelings have been ignored by the pseudo secular rulers. Some people also say that demolition was a mystery and that it was not due to RSS combine.

It was not spontaneous. During the nation wide campaign for the temple, Mr. Advani stated that "Kar Seva will be done with bricks and shovels." Another BJP stalwart Murli Manohar Joshi said "demolish the masjid, nature of Kar Seva will be determined by Sants and not by courts/demolition prerequisite for temple building". Vinay Katiyar: Bajrang Dal Chief went on to say "Masjid will be demolished and debris will be thrown in river Sarayu". Ashok Singhal of VHP was not to be left behind. His resolve was "Decision of *sants* will prevail over decision of legal courts". (The *sants* had already given the call for demolition of the masjid) (Based on Newspaper reports and Mukhopadhayay, 1994)

On the stage Bhajans were sung by Sadhus.

One section of Kar Sevaks beat up journalists and broke their equipment.

* give one more push, demolish the mosque

** This is the beginning, Kashi and Mathura remain to be demolished

As the demolition was going on Kalyan Singh (UP Chief Minister) was advised by Advani not to resign till the demolition is complete.Kalyan Singh accordingly resigned as soon as mosque destruction was complete,simultaneously his government was dismissed by the central government.

P.V. Narsimha Rao, the Prime Minister and Shankarrao Chavan, Home minister could have intervened when the demolition was going on and when post demolition makeshift temple was being built but they preferred to do nothing. Kar Sevaks made the makeshift temple and installed the idols.

"We are sorry to the nation"
7th December, 1992

"It was the will of God"
One week later

"If the sentiments of majority community are not respected, this is what happens"
One month later

Atal Bihari Vajpayee

Bakar Ali

Bakar Ali used to make wooden footwear in Ayodhya, this foot wear was used by devotees visiting the temples. Bakar Ali was thankful to Ram, and Allah was also happy that his follower is able to make his living and is able to pray also in Ayodhya. One day his shop was burnt with all the footwear-- What will happen to the temple goers-
Hey Ram - Kuberdatta.

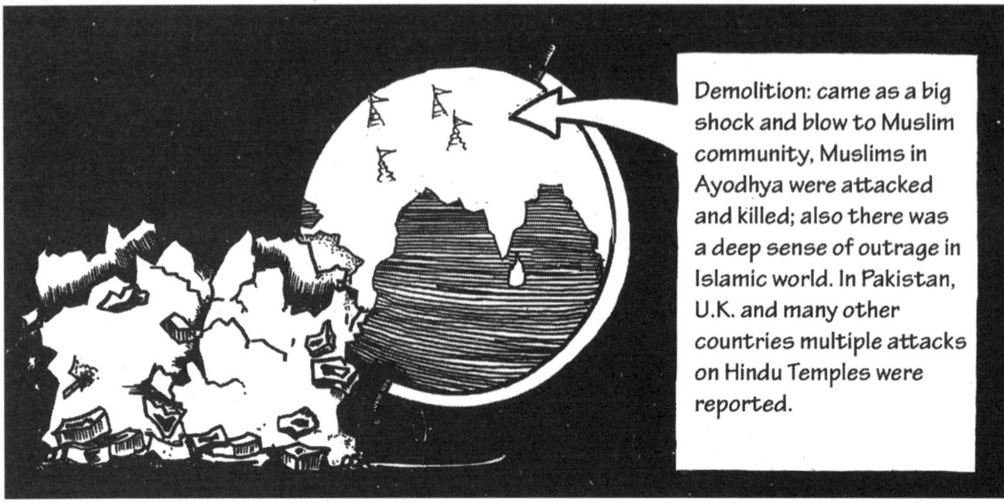
Demolition: came as a big shock and blow to Muslim community, Muslims in Ayodhya were attacked and killed; also there was a deep sense of outrage in Islamic world. In Pakistan, U.K. and many other countries multiple attacks on Hindu Temples were reported.

SURAT
BHOPAL
AYODHYA
MUMBAI
In India communal violence rocked many cities and an atmosphere of social repression was unleashed. The biggest victim of communal violence was Mumbai. Surat, Bhopal, and Ayodhya were other major centers to be affected by this violence. RSS even spread rumour about muslim attacks on temples.

Just be alert, the temple in your area is the next target of Muslims

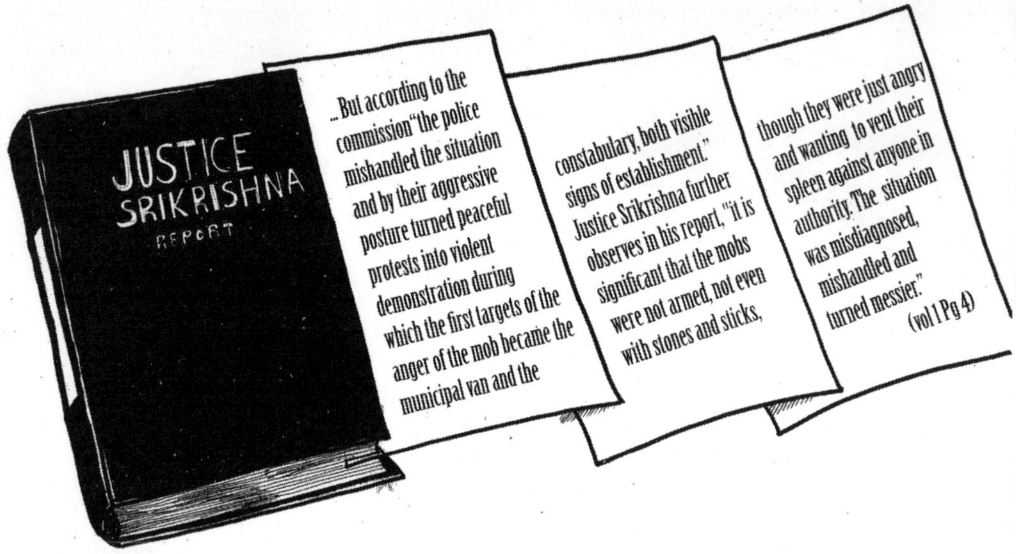

MYTH-As usual in Mumbai also Muslims started the riots and Hindus retaliated.

FACT-It is simplistic and wrong. If we study the events in detail it will be clear that the truth is something else. We will also realise the role of Shiv Sena had been most sinister one, which in this case played the role of the executioner of communal pogrom, and this is more than clear once we go through the report of Justice Shrikrishna.

* Muslims can only be in Pakistan or the graveyard

*Those who attack us will be decimated

Extracts from
'The irresponsible act of Hindutva Parties in celebrating and gloating over demolition of Babri structure was like twisting a knife in the wound and heightened the anguished ire of the Muslims.
The celebration rally organised by Shiv Sena in Dharavi jurisdiction is an example 'It further continues. The Muslims protested, and protested angrily on the streets. Large number of Muslims congregated near Minara Masjid in Pydhonie jurisdiction at about 23.20 hours on 6th December 1992 and came out protesting. Even at this stage, if the mobs had been handled tactfully and with sensitivity and by accepted leaders of both communities, the protest would have been peacefully blown over.'
Srikrishna Commission Report

On 7th December some Muslims attacked a police station to show their anger against government's failure to protect the mosque. Police undertook effective firing in which 90 per cent of those killed were Muslims, due to bullet wounds in abdomen, chest and head.

As per the survey of Riot victims by Nirmala Niketan's College of Social Work students, of the 690 households affected, 86 per cent of victims were Muslims, mostly from poor socio-economic strata, daily wage earners, petty self employed, etc.

They fell to police bullets, were stabbed or burnt. During this time Safiya Hospital was attacked and its ambulance was burnt.

Muslim journalists and those writing against Hindu communalism were preferred targets. Mobs attacking Muslims was generally left unharmed by police.

Shiv Sena procession threw cow dung on mosques, in retaliation Muslims stoned the temples. Riots in Dharavi: Hundreds of houses were destroyed of which 80% were Muslim households. Riots spread to South Bombay and other suburbs.
The worst incident in Surat took place in Vijay Nagar No.2, where 10 feet high bamboo wall was erected to prevent Muslims from fleeing. Flood-lights were installed, nearly 250 Muslim houses were looted and burnt by a well armed mob of around 800 people, who raped the Muslim women and forced them to walk naked under the floodlights. It is alleged that rapes were videotaped. Riots left 246 dead.
In Madhya Pradesh-especially in Bhopal, 120 died as Bajrang Dal celebrated demolition. The scattered violence left a heavy death toll: 259 (Maharashtra: excluding Bombay), 100 (Assam), 201 (UP) 32 (West Bengal), 48 (Rajasthan), 24 (Bihar) and12 (Kerala and Andhra each).

Initial quietness after phase I was marked only by occasional bout of violence. This phase was preceded by intense anti Muslim rumours
Maha Arti was invented and started to mobilise Hindus, Maha Artis aggravated communal tension.
Muslims are preparing to attack with the help of Pakistan and Muslim countries, milk has been poisoned, they are using AK 47s to attack police
A shipload of terrorists are going to land at Dadar Chowpatty, with arms and ammunitions etc.
MAHA ARTI
Many a times Maha Artis were followed by communal violence and exodus of Muslim families of the area.
Between 26-12-1992 to 5-1-1993, 33 Maha Artis were organised.

"The Maha Artis were started from 26th December 1992 and kept adding to the communal tension and endangering the fragile peace which had been established. Some (were used to deliver) communally inciting speeches and the crowds dispersing from (them) indulged in damage, looting and arson of Muslim establishments in the vicinity. (Volume1, page 13)
On 1st January 1993 there was an article in Samna under the caption Hindunni Akramak Vhayala Have,(Hindus should become aggressive now) openly inciting Hindus to violence. (Volume 1 page 13)
सामना
हिन्दूननी आक्रमक
व्हयाला हवे
Low scale, sporadic violence against Muslims continued all through. Two events, blamed on Muslims, in which Hindus were killed, gave the much-needed "legitimacy" to the unleashing of full-fledged anti-Muslim pogroms:
(a) 5th Jan 1993 murder of two Hindu mathadi workers (probably a case of union rivalry) any way there was no proof of being killed by Muslims except the fact that those killed were Hindus.
(b) Jan 8: Bane family's house in Radhabai Chawl: Jogeshwari was burnt: family burnt alive: This as probably a real-estate dispute.
Shiv Saniks are doing the job, Let them carry on
The police was very supportive to rioters and the Shiv Sena mobs. The police justified its soft attitude to anti-Muslim rioters .

In both these cases since the victims were Hindus it got attributed to Muslims; and the much-needed pretext, legitimisation for wholesale violence was available to the Hindu communal forces. Police was very supportive to rioters, Shiv Sena mobs went on rampage.
On the pretext that they have been criticised for their 'shooting sprees' in Dec., police justified its soft attitude to anti-Muslim rioters by saying, 'so now we will not indulge in shooting'. Sena activists were active even before Mathadi & Bane killings. Maha artis were organized to mobilize middle class people. Rumours were circulated that arms are coming from Muslim countries
and that temples were being destroyed in the city. Elaborate planning was done like marking the Muslim houses, establishments and taxis. The Bane family killing and Mathadi killings were used as pretexts to galvanize the Shiv Sainiks into communal violence. The communal violence was followed, after a lapse of few months by serial bombings in which major damage to life and property took place in stock exchange building, Air India building, Worli area and Hotel Sea rock. The plot behind this has not been unearthed but it is suspected
that ISI and Dawood Ibrahim, a noted underworld don planned this. It is interesting to note that while those who indulged in communal violence have not been booked so far, a number of Muslims with slightest suspicion were put behind the bars under TADA, as the probable culprits in serial bombings.
TADA

On 4th January 1993 a big mob of Hindus led by Shri Gajanana Kirtikar, Shri Ramesh More and other Shiv Sena activists took a Morcha. The people in the morcha attacked Chacha Nagar Masjid and the Muslims in the vicinity and injured them. Several Muslim huts in Magdum Nagar in Mahim jurisdiction were set on fire by the Hindus.(Volume 1, page 13-14)

On 7 January 1993 A taxi in which two Muslims were travelling was set on fire in Pratiksha Nagar Antop Hill jurisdiction, resulting in two Muslims being burnt alive. [Volume 1, page15]

On 8 January 1993 some Hindu residences in Radhabai chawl in Jogeshwari jurisdiction were locked from outside and set on fire by miscreants. One male and five female members of a Hindu family and their neighbours were charred to death and three other Hindus sustained serious burn injuries. This incident was sensationalised by the media in giving exaggerated and provoking reports. [Volume1, page15]

From the conversation which could be heard [by Yuvraj Mohite, Mahanagar Reporter, at Thackray house during the riots], it is clear thatThackeray was directing Shiv Sainiks, Shakha Pramukhs and other activists of Shiv Sena to attack the Muslims, [vol.ii, Page 173-174] The Commission does not accept the theory that the January phase of rioting was merely a backlash of the Hindus because of the stabbing, Mathadi worker incidents and the Radhabai chawl incident. "There were attacks going on in the 12 to 15 December 1993 period against Muslims and their properties. Several stabbing incidents carried out by professional criminals with the intention of whipping up communal frenzy in which the majority of the victims happened to be Hindus... the communal passions of the Hindus were aroused to a feverish pitch by the inciting writings, particularly in Samna and Navakal.

* Derogatory word for muslims

[Volume 1, page 21-22]

Bal Thackeray's interview to Time Magazine

(From Communalism Combat, March,1995)

15% SALE
BENNETT, COLEMAN & CO. LTD. | ESTABLISHED 1838 | TIMESOFINDIA.COM | EPAPER.TIMESOFINDIA.COM MUMBAI | SATURDAY, MAY 2, 2009 | PAGES 34
THE TIMES OF INDIA
(On 13th March 1993)
15 powerful explosions rocked the city in areas like, stock exchange, Air India building, Hotel Searock etc. Most of these were placed in cars, while some of them were in scooters also. They left 257 people dead and around 1400 injured. The suspects were those having links with the underworld.
BOOMMMMMMMMMMMM
Dawood Ibrahim appeared to be the kingpin.
Over 200 Muslims arrested under POTA
The Srikrishna Commission which was investigating Mumbai riots was also told to incorporate the blasts also in the arena of investigation. Since special TADA court had been hearing the cases not much was added on the issue by the Srikrishna Commission. The judgement has been delivered (September 2006) in most of the cases and those found guilty have been given punishment. At the same time the guilty of the Mumbai carnage have not been given any punishment. Despite promises the Congress-NCP Government has been dodging the issue and has not taken any worthwhile steps to punish the guilty.

WHO STARTS RIOTS

By now it has been propagated successfully that Muslims start the riots and then Hindus retaliate. Teesta Setalvad (Who Casts the First Stone, Communalism Combat, March' 98) by citing the extracts from five commissions of inquiry shows that truth is the other way around. Following are some of the extracts from the said piece."There was deliberate attempt to suppress the truth from the commission especially the active participation in riots of some RSS and Jan Sangh leaders"(Jana Sangh is the previous political avatar of present BJP) (from Justice Jagmohan Reddy Commission).

"In his report to his superior the SP, Thane district has stated, "I found that " a section of Hindu elements, particularly RSS and some PSP men, were bent upon creating mischief. Their idea in accompanying the procession was not so much to pay respect to the Great Shivaji but to establish the right and, if possible, to provoke and humiliate Muslims. The villagers shouted provocative anti-Muslim slogans, behaved aggressively, threw on the Moti Masjid at Bangad galli Hyderi mosque situated at the junction of Dargarch Road and Sutar Alli aided by passive police." (Justice D.P. Madon Commission).

"In Tellichery, Hindus and Muslims were living as brothers for centuries... It was only after RSS and the Jana Sangh set up their units and began activities in Tellicherry that there came a change in situation. Their anti-Muslim propaganda, its reaction on the Muslims who rallied around their communal organisation, the Muslim league.... the communal tension that followed prepared the background for these disturbances".
(Report of Justice Joseph Vithayathil Commission)

From Report of Commission of Inquiry: "In the run up to the communal build up before the elections prepared by the Intelligence branch, Jamshedpur (March 23, 79) there was a special mention made to the divisional conference of the RSS scheduled to be held on March 31 and April 1, in which among others RSS Sarsangh chalak was to participate. The dispute on route of the procession became sharp and agitated reactions from a group of persons who called themselves Samyukta Bajarang Bali Akhara Samiti, who systematically distributed pamphlets to heighten communal feeling and had organisational links with the RSS. A call for defiance of authority and administration when it refused permission for one of the routes led to violent mob protesting and raising anti-Muslim slogans. Thereafter incendiary leaflets doing rounds of Jamshedpur (issued on behalf of Sri Ramnavmi Kendriya Akhara Samiti), that is nothing short of an attempt to rouse the sentiments of Hindus to a high pitch to distort events and show some actions as attacks on Hindus that appear to be part of a design".

Justice Venugopal Commission:
"RSS methodology for provoking communal violence is:

a. Rousing communal feelings in the majority community by propaganda that Christians are not loyal citizens of this country;
b. Deepening the fear in the majority community by a clever propaganda that the population of minorities is increasing and that of Hindus is decreasing;
c. Training young people of the majority community in the use of weapons like daggers, swords, spears; and
d. Spreading rumours to widen the communal cleavage and deepen communal feelings by giving a communal colour to a trivial incident.

Burning of a bogey of
Sabarmati train
was an act planned by,
International terrorism,
ISI and local Muslims.
-Narendra Modi

On 27th of February the bogey S-6 of Sabarmati train got burnt, the fire killing fifty-eight unfortunate lives. There are different conflicting versions of the episode. The minimum, which can be inferred before the true facts come out from the inquiry commission report are that the bogey was full of Ram Sevaks returning from the pilgrimage to Ayodhya where different rituals around Ram Shila Puja were going on.

Many a reports pointed to the provocative behaviour of Bajrang Dal volunteers traveling in the train. (Jan Morcha, 25th Feb. 2002).

On Godhra platform also the Muslim tea stall vendor was humiliated. One Muslim girl was being forcibly taken by the Kar Sevaks but was rescued.The district collector Jayanthi Ravi stated that the tragedy was unplanned.

He also called a meeting of top Gujarat officials late on 27th and told them...

Sixty two local persons including 7 boys were arrested under POTO.

BANNERJEE COMMISSION ON GODHRA TRAIN BURNING

After two and a half years of the tragic incident, Justice U.C. Bannerjee came out with the truth of Godhra. According to the interim report of the commission, this tragedy was a mere accident and was not a preplanned one as claimed by Narendra Modi and the RSS combine. During the NDA regime, dictated by the RSS combine, the mandatory commission to inquire this major accident was not appointed.

The Gujarat riots were spontaneous act of revenge by Hindus.

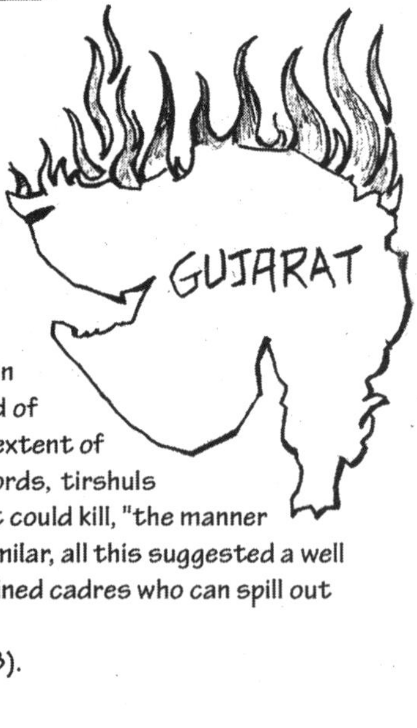

Immediately from the next day, 28 February, massive riot, nay genocide of Muslims began in different cities of Gujarat. Ahmedabad was the major city to be affected. Out of 24 districts of Gujarat, 18 were involved in the violence. Mobs generally comprised of 2000-3000 and sometimes to the extent of 10000 also. They were armed with swords, tirshuls (trident) and agricultural implements that could kill, "the manner of arson, hacking and killing was chillingly similar, all this suggested a well laid out plan behind the attack. It is only trained cadres who can spill out such violence in an organized fashion," (Communalism Combat, March 2002, p. 18).

The household and business establishments of minorities which were burnt during the violence were those whose lists were available with rioters. Even the business establishments, which had Hindu sounding names but had Muslim ownership, came under the attack.

Majority of business establishments owned by Muslim community were destroyed. The household and business establishments were burnt by using gas cylinders and special powder, which raises the temperature to great extent.

In the loot of business establishments large sections of middle classes merrily participated and the looting was coordinated on mobile phones, people came even in their Mitsubishi lancers to do their bit in the service of Hindu Nation by looting the Muslim establishments.

In the industrial area of Ahmedabad 43 people including ex-MP Ahsan Jaffery were killed by a mob of over 10,000 and same evening a mob of over 15,000 killed 84 people in Naroda area.

The victims of violence are estimated to be over two thousand. It was not just killings, those who were killed were subjected to extreme torture. Women and children were the special targets. Women were humiliated and then burnt.

Also under the special attack were places of religious worship more so Dargahs, the symbols of syncretic culture. Many a holy places were destroyed and overnight roads were built on those sites. At places Hanuman temples came up overnight where the mosques or Dargahs were located.

Dargah of famous Gujarati Sufi saint and poet, Wali Gujarati was also not spared. The loss due to burning of business enterprises is estimated to be close to 3800 crores. Hotel, transport, Industry and textile came under special attack.

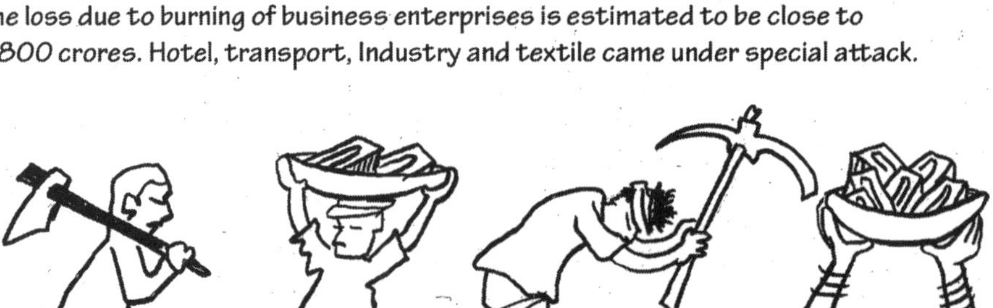

CITIZENS' TRIBUNAL REPORT

Godhra, Gujarat and Akhshardham have been the major blots on our democratic ethos in post Independence India. In the din of the tragedies which gripped Gujarat for over a period of ten months, different versions were floating about "who did it?" The state leadership had one version, while the events themselves were either difficult to decipher on the face value or were indicating the cause of the carnage in some other direction. It is at this point that Concerned Citizens Tribunal was conceived and most outstanding legal brains of the stature of Justices V.K. Krishna Iyer, PB Sawant, Hosbet Suresh, Adv. K.G. Kannabiran, and serious sociologists, Prof. Ghanshyam Shah, Prof. Tanika Sarkar and social workers, Aruna Roy formed this tribunal.

The task was mammoth, the need for knowing the truth paramount and that's what prompted the tribunal members not only to examine 2094 oral and written testimonies, (both individual and collective), from the victim-survivor and Human rights groups involved in relief and rehabilitation. It also examined volumes of relevant material and all this is put together in two volumes, Crimes against Humanity, which in a way is a landmark investigation in situations like these, where vested interests not only try to hide the truth but also to distort the same.

CRIME AGAINST HUMANITY

The findings of the tribunal at one level are close to what many a leading Human Rights activists and scholars were suspecting. The immaculate method of investigation leaves no doubt about the high merit of the report. Its findings point to the complicity of state leadership in the whole tragedy. The tribunal in all its fairness wanted to hear the version of state Govt., Central Govt. and many an individual ministers, who did not respond, while few of them did meet the tribunal and opened their heart.

This two-volume report gives interim findings, also recommendations about relief, rehabilitation and punishing the guilt. But the list of those named by the witnesses is so large that it is practically a 'who is who' of Gujarat political and administrative machinery.

The central point of Godhra, which was made the pretext for the riots, the revenge theory and all that, comes out very clearly in the report. The tribunal concludes that Godhara incident does not seem to be pre-planned. Neither is there a proof of 'foreign hand', which was propagated with confidence. Tribunals' tentative conclusion that the fire was lit from inside and not outside will force us to review the whole, action-reaction thesis, which in a way was used to give legitimacy to state inaction in the face of one of the most severe riots in independent India.

TRUTH OF GUJARAT VIOLENCE

REACTION

The VHP called bandh was fully backed by the BJP and the state. Modi in tune with his being the RSS pracharak was keen to see the consolidation of large section of Hindus behind Sangh Parivar.

In response to the rising anti-Muslim pogrom he said that there is a reaction to every action, and this statement of his went on to encourage the rampaging mobs to no end. In addition, despite evidence to the contrary, he kept on repeating that situation is under control.

In the initial period he even went on to claim that the violence has been brought under control within 72 hours. Nobody bought this claim but his fellow Swayamsevaks sitting in the Home ministry in Delhi patted his back for his 'efficient' work. All the criticism of his policies was deflected by him by asserting that people are defaming the five crore people of Gujarat.

Many a ministers of Gujarat personally went to the police control room to ensure that the rioting mob was let free to do what it is doing, to ensure that the mob is not controlled in anyway.
Many of them led the mobs, Gujarat ministers Nitin Patel and Narav Laloo Patel allegedly led violence against women in Kadih and Unja in Mehasana respectively.

(CC, March 2002, 109).

The *Govt.*'s callous attitude towards this also manifest from the fact that Modi visited the biggest camp 'Shah Alam', only when Vajpayee paid visit to Gujarat, a good two months after the whole tragedy began. Close to a lakh persons living in the camps braved it without bare minimum necessities.

The examination centers of majority community students were shifted away from the minority dominated areas while such a 'care' could not be taken for the students of minority community who had to appear in the examination in such a traumatized state of mind.

The distinction of communities was not spared even in death. The victims of Godhra were to be paid a compensation of Rs. two lakhs while the one's of "retaliatory violence" were to be paid Rs. one lakh. After popular protests and media criticism it was uniformed at one lakh.

The appointment of Justice Shah to investigate the episode also revealed the intentions of the Govt. Justice Shah has the 'reputation' of delivering an anti-Minority judgement in TADA, Dabgarwad- Laliwala, case, which was later reversed by Supreme court. The apex court questioned the very reasoning of the TADA court in convicting the accused. The attitude of the Government filtered down to the civil service. A former cabinet secretary, S R Subramanyam (Indian Express, April 10,2002) went on to say, 'There is no civil service left in Gujarat...Over the years civil service has changed from steel frame to non-existent." This was equally evident in the partisan attitude of police, which not only assisted those conducting the pogroms, but also refused to register the FIR's. Harsh Mander, a civil servant on deputation to Action Aid, was so disgusted after seeing the role of his professional colleagues that he decided to quit the civil service. Also to quit the disgraced service were 20 Muslim officers of ONGC who could tolerate it no longer.

P.C. Pandey summarized the attitude of civil service very well, 'These people also, somehow get carried away by the overall general sentiment. That's the whole trouble. The police are equally influenced by the overall general sentiment'. (CC, March 2002,115).

The rampage, which has been turned, as an upsurge of Hindus by VHP and other RSS affiliates was not spontaneous is also proved by the fact that cranes, trucks and shovels were used extensively for the whole operation. Also the extensive use of gas cylinders, the lists of Muslims household and business enterprises and the import of trucks of swords and dangerous chemicals used commonly also point to the fact of extensive plan which might have gone in to preparation of this pogrom.

A section of media, Sandesh, Gujarat Samachar and their different clones added fuel to the fire by spreading rumours and by carrying these tragedies as sensational headlines. It was to supplement many a poisonous leaflets distributed by different wings of Sangh Parivar.

The most notorious of this was one distributed by VHP calling for a boycott of Muslim business establishments and of Muslim community as a whole.

Many of these called for attacking the Muslims in the name of self-defense, (Reply Bricks with stones, CC March 2002, 136). The training in firearms, distribution of Trishuls (Tridents), which were basically disguised knives, went on unabated, before and during the pogrom.

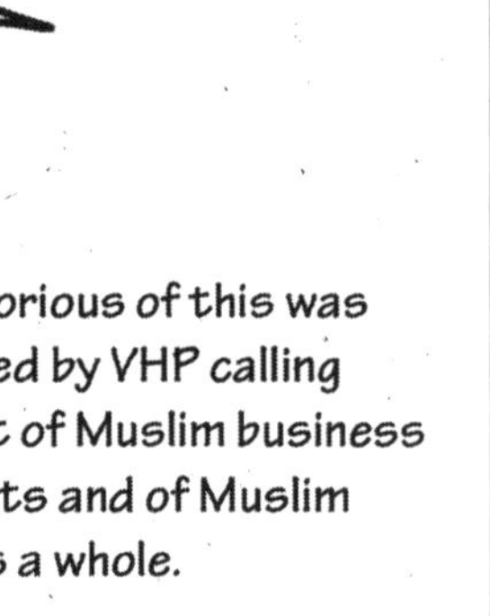

DELIVERENCE OF JUSTICE' in HINDU RASHTRA LABORATORY

Post riot Gujarat again showed the high handedness of its administration. Justice Nanavati was appointed to probe the whole episode. Initially Justice Nanavati went onto state that there was no serious lapse in controlling the communal clashes. He went on to state that there is no evidence against the Bajarang Dal and VHP workers in participating and instigating riots. Best Bakery case witnesses turned hostile, under pressure from the local BJP-VHP workers. Some poor Muslims were made to depose in camera and also in heavy presence of police officials praising the role of police in protecting them.

The PUCL-Vadodara Shanti Abhiyan boycotting the commission and a delegation led by senior Gujarat journalist and Human Rights activist Digant Oza submitting a memorandum drawing the attention of NHRC to the gross violation of human rights of minorities in Gujarat and of the need to restrain the Gujarat Govt. in its acts of commission and omission in the violations of the very elementary democratic rights of minority communities.

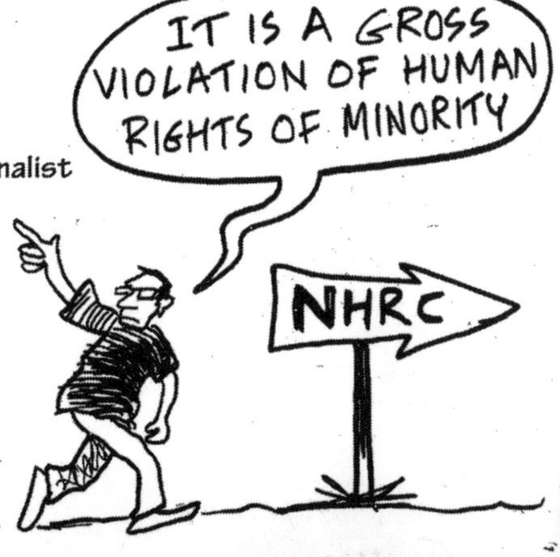

After the riots the local people place a condition to the Muslims that they will be allowed to return to their homes if they withdrew the FIRs in case they have been filed and with an undertaking not to file the FIRs. The civic groups and citizens' tribunal showed without any doubt the role of state machinery and police in aiding and abetting the riots. It was a state sponsored riot so to say. As the state is totally in the grip of Sangh Parivar, the wall of hatred is sealing the borders between the two communities and boycott of Muslims in employment and trade is being close to total. It is in this situation that police finds it easy to tutor the witnesses. Best Bakery witness turning back on their earlier statement was a result of all these factors.To begin with a simple realization that in such a ghettoized atmosphere it may not be possible to socially survive while giving the witness against the authorities and the political elements. Secondly a more direct threat from different sources is regularly threatening the victims to keep shut. The Vadodara episode where police has taken the witnesses to depose is the best example of travesty of justice.

Zahira Shiekh

Supreme Court has saved the democracy in this adverse scenario. Its observation that Gujarat Govt. has not done its duty in prosecuting the guilty of the riots came as a big slap to Modi who so far had been behaving like a rampaging bull. Its judgement to get the cases of Zahira Shiekh heard again with due protection is a landmark.

Tehelka Expose, Nov 2007

(From the Special issue 3rd November 2007)

The sting investigation conducted by Tehelka magazine showed the guilty of the riots boasting of their crimes on the camera.

* Modi visited Godhra on 27th and his outburst provided the first sign to Sangh workers that time to corner Muslims has come.

* That very night BJP and Sangh workers met at Ahmedabad, Vadodara and Godhra, and gave the green signal for an all out assault on Muslims across the state.

* A strategy was decided on how to shield the attackers from the law after the riots. Prominent lawyers were briefed and senior police officers taken into confidence. Workers were told that Modi was squarely behind them.

* The mobilization of under castes, something the Sangh has been engaged in for years, dovetailed into the deep penetration of Hindutva already had amongst the upper castes of Gujarat. Godhra provided the perfect spark to fuse them together.

* From the very beginning the police played a very partisan role, often joining the mobs. Officers who tried to do their duty found their hands tied. The complacity was led by then Ahmedabad Commissioner P.C.Pandey who ensured compliance by a swathe of junior officers.

* Weapons from bombs to trishuls, were manufactured and distributed by workers of RSS combine. They were also smuggled by them from all over the country.

* BJP and Sangh leaders led the bloodthirsty mobs through Ahmedabad's bylanes, Sabarkantha's villages, Vadodara's localities. The police stood guard to the mayhem.

* BJP MLA Mayaben Kodnani drove around Ahmedabad's Naroda locality all day directing the mobs. VHP leaders Atul Vaid and Bharat Teli did the same at Gulbarga Housing society. None of them ever went to jail.

* Fire was the most favoured weapon in rioters hands. That cremation is considered un Islamic fuelled their frenzy to burn. Petrol and kerosene were lavishly used, as were victims own gas cylinders.

* Babu Bajrangi reveals that he collected 23 revolvers from Hindus in Naroda Patiya. He called Jaideep Patel 11 times and informed Gordhan Zadaphia the then minister of state for home about the death toll.

* Government counsel before Nanavati-Shah Commission, Arvind Pahdya, himself worships Modi and describes Justice Shah as 'our man'.

INDIAN SOCIETY

SYNCRETIC CULTURE

Indian society has a rich diversity. Starting from arrival of Aryans, there was an interaction-conflict, cooperation and synthesis of different cultural/ religious streams.

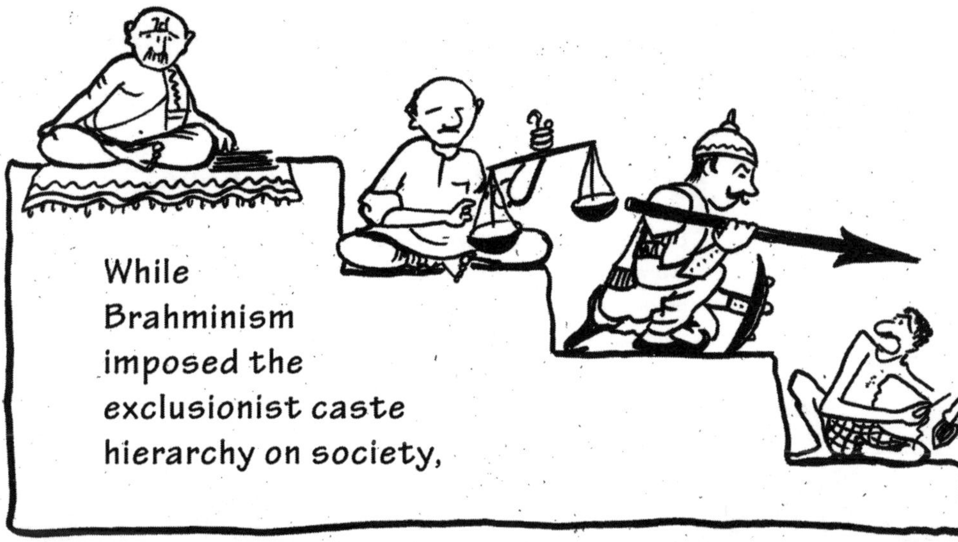

other streams like Jainism, Buddhism, Kabir, Nanak and multiple local sects Jotiba, Khandoba, Tukaram, Chaitanya Mahaprabhu, Tantra contributed to the synthesising of local cultures.

While kings, zamindars and upper castes exploited, irrespective of their religion, the lower castes intermingled and led to the development of syncretic traditions.

MYTH

Indian culture is a Hindu culture. There has been invasion of foreign cultures like Islam and Christianity, which have "attacked" our culture.

FACT

On the contrary, as we will see Indian culture is a plural one, encompassing the diversity of the country, incorporating and drawing heavily from all those people, who came and settled here. Even amongst Hindus there are multiple sects and the culture is not uniform. Only the culture of elite, is being projected to be "the" Hindu culture at the exclusion of the culture of downtrodden.

We will see that there was extensive trade between the Malabar coast and the Arabs. As a matter of fact, Islam first came to India through Arab traders. Many a coastal kings had erected mosques for these traders and for the local Muslim community, evolving through interaction with the Arabs.

Make some arrangement to support all artists and artisans
The arrival of Mughals on the political arena was marked by multiple changes. Like any other rulers Mughals were ruthless exploiters and applied coercion as well as ideological maneuvers to rule. The impact of Islam and the culture of Mughals led to development of a synthesis.

Hindustani culture, in all the fields: music, sculptors, architecture, literature, fine arts and so on. At religious level, Islam and local Hindu traditions interacted and strengthened Sufi Saints and Bhakti Cults, both very popular with subaltern following.

Sufis were more tilted towards spiritual side of Islam. They had to oppose the orthodox Ulema of Islam (learned in Islamic Theology) who were close to the elite and the power center of the society.

These Sufis were close to Christians and Jew mystics and spirituality of some Hindu sects. Moinuddin Ibn Arabi founded the doctrine of Wahadat-Al-Wajud (i.e. Unity of being), this doctrine promoted spiritual universalism and demolished the barriers of caste and creed. According to their preaching 'the real being is one and we are all His manifestations'. Baba Farid of Punjab wrote his poetry in Punjabi and his verses were quoted in the Adi Granth Saheb by Gurunanak.

Mir Miyan, another Sufi saint was requested to lay the foundation stone of Harmandir in golden temple. Sayyid Waris Shah wrote Hir Ranjha, greatest classic of medieval Punjabi literature.

Nizamuddin Awliya was another major sufi saint. One day he was passing through bank of Jamuna in Delhi, accompanied by his celebrated disciple and noted poet, Khoosro. They saw some Hindu women bathing in Jamuna and offering prayer to the Sun. Hazrat said...

Sheikh Moinuddin Chishti was a great Sufi saint with large following. While Ulemas and Brahmins looked down upon other's mode of worship, Sufi and Bhakti Saints modified and integrated these modes into a new synthetic stream. They respected other's spiritual practices, and were away from power centers. Dara Shikoh was a great scholar and he wrote a book called Majama-ul-Baharayn (meeting of two great oceans, Hinduism and Islam)

PHOOLWALON KI SAIR

Even though many Muslims celebrated Diwali and Holi, Hindus participated in Id and Moharrum, Phoolwalon Ki Sair was one Delhi festival in which Hindus and Muslims participated alike. During the reign of Akbar Shah, Bahadur Shah Zafar's younger brother Mirza Jahangir, once happened to insult the British Resident Sten. The Resident had the prince arrested and sent to Allahabad. it was feared that Mirza Jahangir might not come back alive. His mother, Nawab Mumtaz Mahal prayed at the dargah of Khwaja Qutubuddin Bakhteyar Kaki, that if her son got released she would offer a Chaparkhat (bed of flowers) to the tomb. A few days later Sten himself issued order to free the prince. When Badshah Begum, Mumtaz Mahal went to present her offering at the Dargah, almost all Hindus and Muslims participated in the procession. Since then it was decided that every year Muslims should offer a pankha at the Dargah and Hindus, at the Jog Maya Mandir. Thus both Hindus and Muslims participated in the two ceremonies with great enthusiasm. Thereafter every year, the residents of Delhi proper would shift to Mehroli and camp there for 8 to 10 days. The festivities saw all sorts of entertainments including dance performances by tawaifs. Of late, mela at the Dargah as well as the Jog Maya Mandir has been revived but its importance is nothing more than symbolic.

MYTH

Indian literature is contribution of Hindus alone.

FACT

This notion has nothing to do with the truth. Literature also witnessed synthetic trends. Baba Farid wrote in Punjabi, and was amongst the founders of Punjabi poetry. Shaikh Mohammed wrote Marathi poetry. Guru Ramdas was all praise for Sheikh Mohhamed about whom he wrote...

"Glory to Shaikh Mohammad You alone unfold the mystery of the universe in such diction that baffles the reason and logic of ordinary mortals. You have truly perceived the fundamental unity and identity of the entire universe."

Malik Mohamad Jaysi was a great poet of Avadhi and wrote the classic "Padmavat". Abdur Rahim Khan-e-Khana- was a Hindi poet in the court of Akbar.

तै रहीम मन आपुनो, कीन्हों चारू चकोर ।
निसिबासर लाग्यो रहै, कश्णचंद्र की ओर ।।

रहिमन यहि संसार में, सब सों मिलिए थाइ ।
ना जैनै कोहि रूप में, नारायण मिलि जाइ ।।
रहीम

I have transformed my soul into a bird Chakor who keeps looking at Lord Krishna out of devotion In this world we should meet all the people with love, you never know in whose form you come across Narayan(God).

Ras Khan made great contributions to Hindi poetry and wrote songs in praise of Lord Krishna. Mazhar Jan-i-Jana said that Bedas (Veda) were the revealed book of God, Ram and Krishna must have been prophets of God. Ramanand founded the Bhakti movement, propounded the devotion to Ram and threw open the doors of his circle to all the low caste men and women and also to Muslims.

Tulsidas was ardent Rambhakta, in fact the greatest Ram Bhakta of all the times. He wrote his literature not in Sanskrit but in popular Avadhi language, so that it could be accessible to all the people. Because of this he was not well accepted amongst his peers. He used to live in Ayodhya in a Mosque.

MYTH

Hindus and Muslims kept aloof and were hostile to each other.

FACT

This is contrary to the truth. It is true that elite of the communities for their vested interests looked down upon the other communities and other's religions. But the poor of both the communities flocked to the holy seers irrespective of their religion. Kabir had a large following amongst the poor from amongst Muslims as well as Hindus. He criticised the orthodoxy of Ulema and Brahmins both and pointed out that Ram, Rahim, Allah and Hari are the expressions of the same spiritual energy. As different ornaments are made from the same gold so are these holy seers.

'तुलसी' गुलाम सरनाम है राम को,
जाको रूचै सो कहे कछु वोहू।
मांग के खयिबो, महजिद मा रहिबो,
लेबै का एक न देबै का दोऊ ।।
तुलसी

Tulsi is slave of Ram, whatever they may say, let them say. On alms I live, the mosque is my refuge, my give and take with this world is done.

Kabir occupies a very high position among the poets, spiritualists and philosophers of India. While the exact date and place of his birth is not known, the majority of scholars believe that he was born in Belahara village in Azamgarh (U.P.) in the last decade of the 15th century.

कुलकानि हियो जति भाजति है....
कल कानन कुडंल मोरपखा
उर पै बनमाल बिराजति है।
मुरली कर में अधरा मुसकनि
तरंग महाछवि छाजति है।।
रसखानि तन पीतपटा
सत दामिनी की दुति लाजित है।
वह बांसुरी की धुनि कानि परें,
कुलकानि हियो तजि भाजति है।।
रसखान

Ras Khan made great contribution to Hindi poetry. See this poem of his written in praise of Lord

Guru Nanak founded new religious movement blending the concept of Unity of God, which was closely allied to Islamic concept with Hindu doctrine of rebirth, moral and spiritual reform.

Abul Fazal in Ain-e-Akbari wrote that the king should be above all religious differences and see that religious considerations do not come in the way of duty, which he owes to every class and every person. Under his all-embracing care everyone should find peace and happiness so that the benefits conferred by the shadow of God are universal.

Urdu is a foreign language and all the Muslim invaders either used Urdu or Persian

On the contrary Urdu was a language, which came up as an interaction of Persian and Hindi. It is a language, which is a mixture of Persian dialect with western Hindi spoken in and around Delhi. The interaction produced a dialect called as Hindavi, Hindi, or Hindustani, later called as Urdu. Raja Todarmal, Akbar's finance minister ordered all the accounts and correspondence to be kept in Persian. Mullah Abdul Kadir Badaunni in cooperation with Hindu pundits translated Athrva Veda and Ramayana in Persian. Greatest writers of Persian in Medieval India were Abul Fazal, Aurangzeb, Munshi Harakram, Chandrabhan Brahman, and Munshi Madhav Ram.

Mughal style is a mix of Persian and Hindu styles. Mughal or Hindustani style is seen in palaces of Raja of Chatarpur, memorials of Ranjit Singh [Lahore], and Maharaja Bakhtavar Singh [Alwar]. In Mughal states there was dominance of Persian in govt. offices, however large number of employees were Hindus. Department of literary skills, Dar-ul-insha [secretariat] was mainly having Hindus during 18th century. Word Munshi stands for a Hindu who could write good Persian.

हमने बनाए यदि अजंता–एलोरा–कोणर्क
तो उन्होने भी बनाए ताजमहल, कुतुबमीनार, चारमीनार,
हमने दिए कालिदास, बाणभट्ट, रवींद्रनाथ
तो उन्होंने भी दिए खुसरो, गालिब, फिराक
हमने दिए जयदेव, कुमार गंधर्व, भीमसेन जोषी, जसराज
तो उन्होंने भी दिए बड़े गुलाम अली खान,
बिस्मिल्ला खान, डागर बंधु
हमने दिए सहगल, हेमंत, मन्ना, लता
तो उन्होंने भी दिए रफी, नूरजहां, नौषाद
हमने दिए अवनीद्रनाथ,नंदलाल बसु, रवि वर्मा,
अमश्ता षेरगिल
तो उन्होंने भी दिए हुसैन, रजा, आरा
और जहां तक देष की आजदी की बात है
या षहादत की,
तो हमारे तात्या,लक्ष्मी, मंगल पांडे, गांधी,
नेहरू, सुभाश, भगत सिंह, चंद्र षेखर, रामप्रसद
के साथ ही खड़े है उनके भी ज़फर, टीपू, बेगम हजरतमहल,
अबुल कलाम, अषफाक , अब्दुल हमीद
.... आलोक भट्टाचार्य

If we made Ajanta-Ellora-Konark
Then they also have built Tajmahal,
Kutubminar, Charminar
We gave Kalidas, Banbhatta, Ravindranath,
They also gave Khusaro, Ghalib, Firaq.
We gave Jayadev, Kumar Gandharva, Bhimsen
Joshi, Jasraj,
They gave Bade Ghulam Ali Khan,
Bismilla Khan
Dagar Bandhu.
We gave Sehgal, Hemant, Lata,
They gave Rafi, Noorjahan, Naushad.
We gave Avanindranath, Nandlal Basu,
Ravi Varma, Amrita Shergil,
They also gave Husain, Raza, Aara.
As far as freedom struggle of martyrdom
is concerned
Alongwith our Tatya, Laxmi, Mangal Pande,
Gandhi, Nehru, Subhash, Bhagat Singh,
Chandrashekar are standing,
Their Jafar,Tipu, Hazaratmahal, Abdul Kalam,
Ashraf, Abdul Hamid.
--Alok Bhattacharta

Our Mixed Heritage

The most prominent element of the Heritage of a nation is its culture. The culture of a nation finds expression in two ways: the visible elements are dresses worn by the people, the food they eat, music, dance and architecture. The invisible elements are the way people think, the values they hold dear and their ideas and beliefs.

Culture is not something that has been there from time immemorial, it is also not something that is frozen in time. Culture is in fact something that is dynamic and constantly changing, it absorbs new influences, and modifies them to suit local requirements, it constantly appropriates from other traditions and also gives to them in equal measure. It has always been so and it will continue to be like this as long as human beings live.

Almost everything that we see, taste, hear, smell and touch, the buildings we have built, the tools we use, the clothes we wear, the languages we speak and even the ideas that we have are products of processes, discoveries, inventions and developments that occurred at places far and near in times in the distant and not so distant past and have reached us through very complex and roundabout routes.

Let us look at some of the more mundane elements of our daily lives that we do not normally consider as part of our culture but they are as important as our classical traditions in dance and music. We refer here to our attire. This may come as a shock but nothing that is stitched is Indian. The Shirt, The Trouser, The Coat, The Waist Coat are all of European origin.
What about the Payjama? The word is of Persian origin it means a garment worn over the legs. The Kurta is probably from the same region or from Afghanistan.
The Shalwaar Kameez came to us probably from Afghanistan, but it is possible that the Kameez is Portuguese/ Turkish in its origin. The Chemise, an undergarment worn by women is of French origin, the Blouse is English and so is the Peticoat. The last three have no word for them in any Indian language.
In fact as recently as the late 19th century when the Brahmo-Samaj in Bengal started a campaign in Bengal that women should cover the upper part of their body by wearing the blouse, there were vociferous protests from organizations of Bengali Brahmins lamenting the fact that the blouse was part of a European conspiracy against our traditions and culture.

A piece of cloth that has been cut with scissors was considered unwhole - kshit as opposed to akshit, and therefore impure. In fact most rituals related to birth, death and Upnayan among the Hindus and even among the Jains and Boudhs are performed in unstitched garments and even today a very large majority of our population primarily dresses up in unstitched garments - Dhoti, Lungi, Mundu, Saree. We had no stitched garments before the Kushanas and the Greeks probably brought the scissors to us.

Taj Mahal's soaring facades are an example of the subtle blending of Islamic and Hindu ideas. White marble, rather than the red sandstone used by former Muslim rulers for their palaces and forts, was chosen as the material by Shah Jahan, who had been impressed by the beauty of the white marble buildings he had seen in Delhi and Rajasthan.

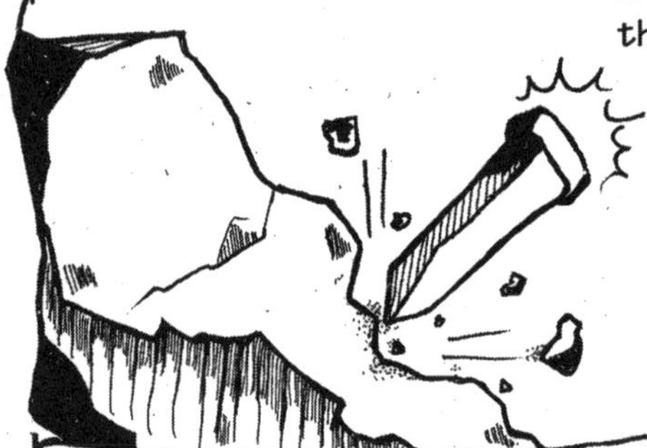

Pointed arches of Muslim inspiration frame windows and doors, in which are set perforated marble grilles of the type often found in Hindu temples. The arabesques and chevrons on the outside are Muslim patterns, but here they take the form of semi-precious stones inlaid in the marble, a technique imported from Italy and mastered by Hindu artisans.

Communalism : Rise and Growth

MYTH

5000

Ours is a five thousand year old Hindu Nation!

FACT

This is a misconception as Nation States are a modern phenomenon. Earlier Kingdoms were the norm. Nation states succeeded the kingdoms first in Europe, nearly four centuries ago. Kings were authoritarian rulers; with network of feudal lords, and agriculture was the main production.

Nascent crafts got organised as guilds and later into industry. Nation states generally, though not always are democratic formations based on Liberty, Equality and Fraternity.

Those nations, which industrialized earlier went out to colonize other countries, especially in Asia, Africa and South America. India was colonized mainly by British, small portions by Portuguese and French. British 'plunder project' aimed at taking away the raw materials from here and creating markets for their goods. In order to do these, they set up new ventures here in agrarian, commercial and industrial arenas.

In these, Indians first acted as subordinates but soon took to modern technologies and with this a new class of merchants, bankers, landlords, industrialists, plantation owners and brokers came into being. Introduction of English education in 1835 was meant to produce a class of clerks and administrators. This changing social dynamics laid the foundation of the new phenomenon of 'nationalism'. In a very elementary form this changed scenario formed the backdrop for rise of different reform movements and new associations and unions of economic, social and political nature on the western pattern. In due course, the intelligentsia started demanding widening of franchise, simultaneous examinations for administrative services, Indianization of services.

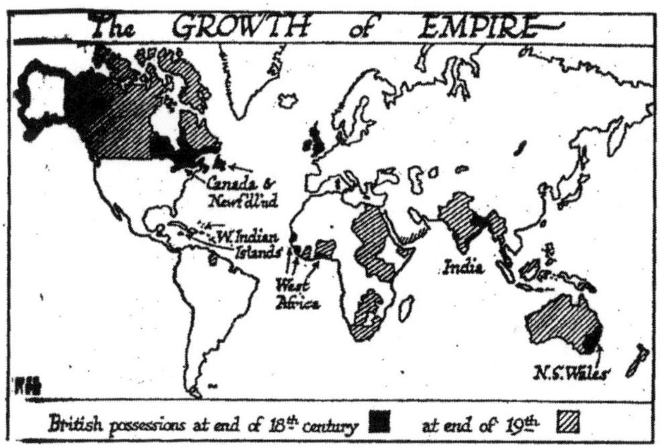

And in this demand of theirs emerging industrialists supported them adding their own demands for increased facilities for industrialization in India. A spirit of Indian consciousness started emerging for the first time and this was due to a combination of various factors like material demands of newly emerging classes (professionals, businessmen, industrialists).

Modern
education,
communication
(railways, telegraphs, free press,
hatred for British racial arrogance,
economic exploitation, weaknesses of judiciary were some of the features of the changes occurring at that time. British rule and the process unleashed by them were pregnant with contradictory processes. Free press created a strong impetus for the rise of national consciousness. This led to the formation of many local regional associations aimed at voicing the grievances of emerging elite and projecting their vision of 'nation'.

These associations, the Bombay association, Madras natives association, Pune Sarvajanik Sabha and Madras Mahajan Sabha. The major meeting of these associations started taking place and the one such which took place in Calcutta in 1883 was the precursor of the formation of the INC (Indian National Congress) in 1885.

Indian National Congress expressed the ambitions of these associations and rising classes and asked . . .

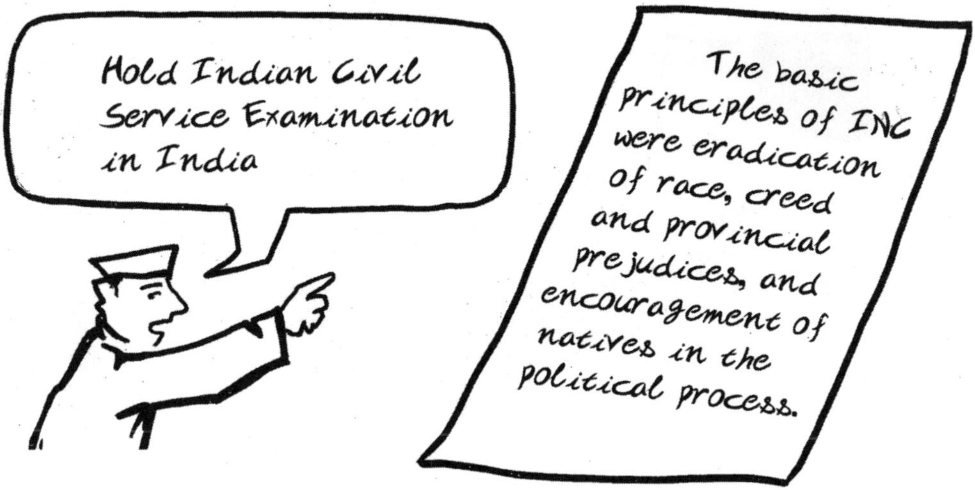

In response to this, Sir Syed and Raja Sheo Prasad of Kashi formed United India Patriotic Association (August 1888). The aim of this association was to convey to the British that all communities and aristocracies are not with Congress, to convey the views of Hindu and Muslim organisations to the British Parliament and to strengthen the rule of British in India, to wean away people from Congress. Many a people associated with this association were later to be part of Muslim League and Hindu Mahasabha. The mix of these processes and secular organisation being thrown up was described by Surendranath Banerjee and Lokmanya Tilak as "India is a nation in the making" meaning thereby that it is a representation of common interests of Indian people vis-a-vis the colonial power.

At this time reformers like Rammohan Roy were asking for abolition of abominable practices like Sati. Phule at this time was calling for taking to modern education and women's education. Savitribai Phule and Pandita Ramabai took up the cause of women's education.

Phule also laid the foundation of a Non-Brahmin movement aimed against the social power of Zamindar-Brahmin nexus. Later Ambedkar was to pick up the threads of this movement and struggle for the rights of the untouchables .

Rise of communalism has been a very complex process. Colonial policies generated the growth and economic domination of merchant-money lenders (by and large Hindus). Hindus could take maximum advantage of modern education and accordingly, a place in bureaucracy.

Post 1857 anti Muslim bias of British gave slight edge to Hindus, who took to modern enterprises/professions with great keenness. British Historians used the categories Hindu, Muslim, and Brahmin etc. Indian historians picked up only two of these categories, Hindu and Muslim.

Indian leadership used religious consciousness to inculcate 'Modern nationalism' amongst the people, eg. Ram Rajya, Khilafat. This resulted in two processes:

(a) arousal of nationalism

(b) arousal of communalism.

We will shortly see that communalism arose due to the politics of Muslim feudal lords, Hindu Zamindars and British policy of divide and rule.

Introduction of Education: Industrialization: Changes in Social Values, Relationships

Group A Secular Democratic	Group B Communal
Rise of New classes of Businessmen-Industrialists, Workers, Educated classes	Decline of Landlords, Kings and section of clergy associated with them
These Groups form Associations, Bombay Association, Madras Mahajan Sabha etc.	This groups looks at new changes with fear and suspicion
Their political expression in the form of Indian National Congress	Fearful of the rise of new classes and INC, they form United India Patriotic association UIPA to promote loyalty to British
In due course other political streams expressing the values of this group come up, Hindustan Socialist Republican Association, (Bhagat Singh and Friends), Republican Party of India (Dr Ambedkar)	UIPA gave rise to Hindu Maha Sabha, Muslim League. Later RSS came up as an ideology inspired by leaders of Hindu Maha Sabha
This stream was conceptualizing for India as a nation in the making.	Muslim League held that they are a Muslim Nation since the advent of Mohammad bin Kasim Hindu Maha Sabha/RSS held that We are a Hindu Nation since times immemorial
This group held the values of Liberty, Equality. Equal rights to people of all religions, all caste and both genders	Ideology was based on hierarchy of caste and gender, as sanctified by the organized religion, clergy
Participated in freedom movement and process of social change	Totally aloof from freedom movement and opposed to social change

MYTH

Partition took place due to the Muslim League's ambition and Jinnah played a central role in this.

FACT

Partition was a multi factorial tragedy. In this Muslim communal politics, Hindu communalism and British policy of divide and rule played the central part. Muslim League was representative of the interests of Muslim elite. It wanted to appropriate maximum privileges for the Rich Muslims. It stated that Muslims are 25% of the population, but for passing any legislation 2/3 majority is necessary, Muslims should be granted 1/3 representation in legislatures so that they can prevent anti-Muslim legislations, Congress rejected this demand. Jinnah emerged as the major leader of Muslim League.

Two nation theory was simultaneously accepted by Muslim communalists (Chowdhary Rahmat Ali, Muslim League) and Hindu communalists (Hindu Maha Sabha, RSS). Along with the birth of Congress, began two opposite, but in some way similar, trends which were opposed to the secular politics of Congress. The first of these was expressed by Sir Syed Ahmed, who opened this campaign in 1887, and the second was the Hindu revivalist streams.

THE COMMUNAL TRIANGLE

With the formation of Indian National Congress and its representation of the cause of "rising classes", and its methods of 'protest' vis-a-vis loyalty, he (Sir Syed) got alarmed and kept aloof from this. Instead he set out to organise the Jagirdari elements amongst Muslims, and along with his followers, he propagated that Congress is meant for the interests of the Hindus and 'low born' classes.

In contrast to Congress demand for representation he was for nomination of elite by the British and said that the British are the best guardians of the Muslim interests in India.

Later these efforts culminated in the formation of Muslim league, which stood for the interests of Muslim landlords and Nawabs of Riyasats.

Simultaneously the principles of the Congress were being opposed by another section also. This again was the section of Hindu Zamindars, traditional tradesmen (baniyas) and the Rajas of Riyasats (Princely states).

From 1870's, a section of Hindu zamindars, moneylenders and middle class professionals began to arouse anti-Muslim sentiments, simultaneously opposing the Congress goal of a single nation, of a common nation irrespective of religious identities.

They talked of tyrannical rule of Muslim rulers and of the role of British in giving liberation from that.

They came up with the formulation, that ancient, pre-Mughal age was the golden age of India. The leader of Arya Samaj, Pandit Lekh Ram went on to condemn all forms of Islam and demanded that...

They founded Punjab Hindu Sabha, were hostile to Indian National Congress. According to them INC's role of uniting people of different religions into a single nation meant sacrificing Hindu interests to appease Muslims.

The culmination of these efforts led to the formation of Hindu Maha Sabha and later Rashtriya Swayamsevak Sangh.

BRITISH POLICY OF DIVIDE & RULE

British rulers realised the differences between Hindu and Muslim elite and embarked on the policy of divide-et-empera (divide and rule). With the formation of Indian National Congress, they were very uncomfortable with its demands. Sir Syed's opposition to these demands came in handy for them and they encouraged Sir Syed and his elite followers in their 'communal demands'. British played their cards well and taking advantage of Hindu Muslim divide, they tried to snub the INC time and over again. They recognized a group of Muslim Nawabs and Jagirdars (Shimla delegation) as the representative of Muslims, and similarly encouraged the Hindu Maha Sabha and RSS. None of the organisations undertook any anti-British agitation, neither were they subject of repression by the British.

Thus there are three major factors which resulted in the partition of the country. First was the British policy of 'divide-and-rule'. Second was the Muslim communalism representing the interests of Muslim Zamindars, Nawabs and other elite. The third was the Hindu Communalism (RSS , Hindu Maha Sabha and partly through Congress) which represented the interests of Hindu Zamindars, Brahmins,Baniyas (traditional tradesmen).

TRAGEDY OF INDIA'S PARTITION

Colonial period: decline of Muslim landlords, adverse representation of Muslims in jobs, except in U.P., rise of traders (mainly Hindus), part of colonial commercial bourgeoisie transformed into industrial bourgeoisie.
In 1937 elections Congress came in majority in many states, formed governments , rejected Jinnahs demand for incorporation in ministries, rejected, Jinnah's demands of partition.
Even before this in 1937, Hindu Maha Sabha convention Bhai Parmanand said "Mr. Jinnah argues, there are two nations in the country (Hindus and Muslims), he is right. Congress theory of building a common nationality falls to the ground.
There are only two options
(1) Partition of country
(2) Allow Muslim state to grow in the present state.

Congress leadership left with only two options
(1) strong centre with partition
(2) loose federation without partition.
They opted for (1), despite Gandhi's opposition to this.

Hindu Mahasabha in 1937, Ajmer session 1937 demanded the partition of the country. Most of the Muslim elite was for the same. Muslim elite was represented by Muslim League and demand higher representation with an eye for more privileges. After rejection of this demand they were firm on demand of Pakistan, hoping that this would give them unlimited power avoiding the competition from Hindu elite.

Muslims were 25 per cent of the population. As the franchise was based on property holding or education, only 10 per cent of these were eligible to vote, from amongst these only per cent voted for Muslim League. When the resolution for creation of Pakistan was passed in Lahore convention of Muslim League, many a poor Muslims took out processions condemning this resolution.

Trajectory of events leading to formation of Pakistan

Muslim Communal Politics	Hindu Communal Politics
1860 Sir Syed Ahmed articulates the need for modern education and jobs for Muslims.	Hindu Zamindars and elite demand a share of seats in legislature and call for cow slaughter ban
1906: Formation of Muslim League projecting the fear of Hindu majority. It is mainly a Demand of Muslim elite	1907 - Formation of Punjab Hindu Sabha 1915 - Hindu Maha Sabha formed 1920s - Lala Lajpat Rai: wrote 13 articles saying that Hindus & Muslims can't live together, Bangal & Punjab should be partitioned. 1925: Rashtriya Swayam Sevak Sangh formed
Poet Iqbal: demands separate homeland for Muslims in North West.	Nehru Committee Report, 1927 Nehru Committee under pressure from Hindu Mahasabha rejected the 4 point demand of Muslim League. This formed first base of demand for Pakistan
Chaudhary Rahmat Ali coins the word Pakistan.- P for Punjab, A for Afghans (Pathans), K for Kashmir, S for Sind and Stan the Persian suffix meaning land	1930: Lala Lajpat Rai in a letter to Mahatma Gandhi demands the partition of country. 1933: Bhai Parmanand: President Hindu Maha Sabha calls for cooperation with British to settle the score with Muslims.
1932 -Macdonald's Communal award	1937: Hindu Maha Sabha: Ajmer Session resolution says Hindus and Muslims are two seperate nations
1937 Muslim demand of fighting elections jointly and then participation in the Govt. is rejected by Congress. Jinnah's Two Nation theory takes shape.	1938: Bhai Parmanand: "Mr. Jinnah argues that there are two nations in the country...If Mr. Jinnah is right & I believe he is, then the Congress theory of building common nationality falls to ground. This situation has got two solutions. One is the partition of country into Two & the other to allow Muslim state to grow within the Hindu State"

Cabinet mission plan (1945) Autonomy of States: Unacceptable to Congress. Nehru's stand that forthcoming constituent assembly can change the earlier agreements comes as the final blow to unity efforts. Impasse. Partition proposed by Mountbatten. Acceptance by both Congress and Muslim League

CAUSES OF GROWTH OF COMMUNALISM IN INDIA

A stagnant secularization process (separation of religion and politics) due to:

1. Slow development of economy

2. Competition between Hindu and Muslim elite

3. Weak mercantile bourgeoisie vis-a-vis feudal lords

4. British policy of divide and rule

Muslim League: representatives only of Muslim elites. People like Khan Abdul Gaffar Khan, Hakim Ajmal Khan, Dr. Ansari, Maulana Abul Kalam Azad stood for secular nationalism, Hindu Muslim unity, and anti-British struggles. Maulana Hussain Ahmed Madani : 'These days nations are based on 'Geographical boundaries and not on religion'.

IInd WORLD WAR

Most elite (bureaucrats, businessman and rich landlords) left for Pakistan. Most of those left behind - poor, landless, self employed artisans etc. were not the ones asking for Pakistan. After partition, the Muslim community shrunk in size, subdued, started being blamed for partition.

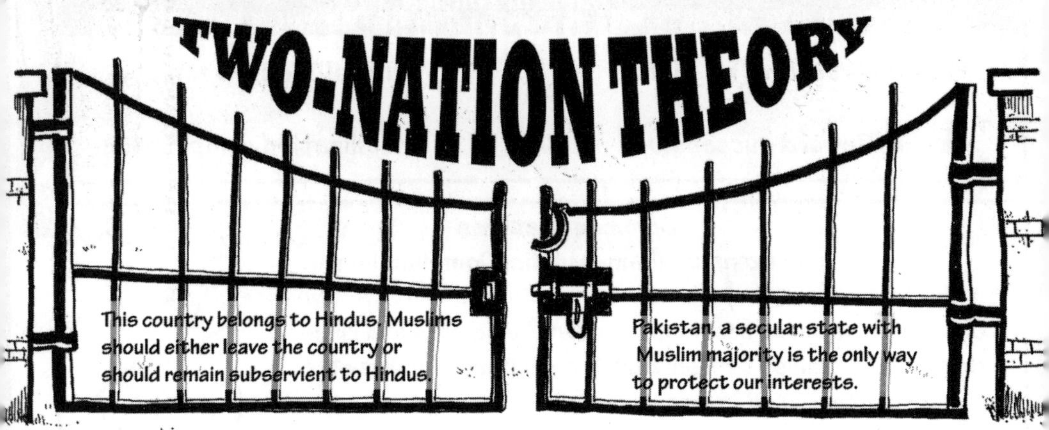

What is Communalism ?

A belief or ideology according to which all people belonging to one religion have common economic, social and political interests and these interests are contrary to the ones of those belonging to another religion. There are three stages (degrees), discernible in the development of Communalism:

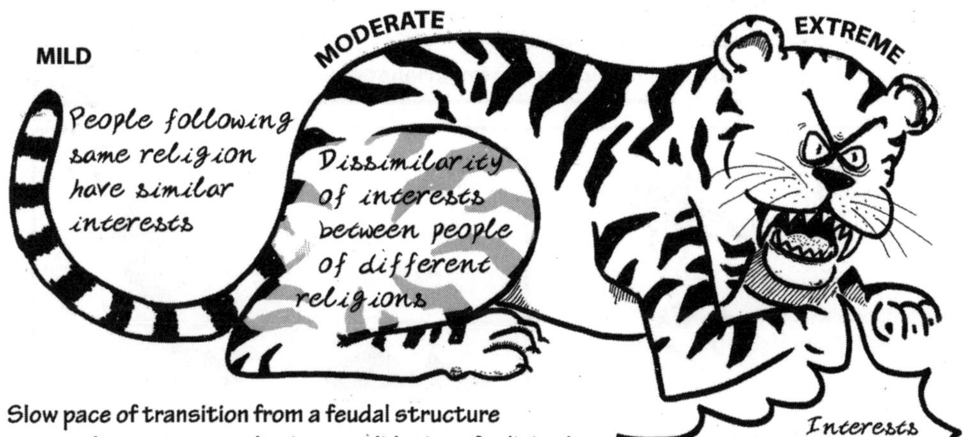

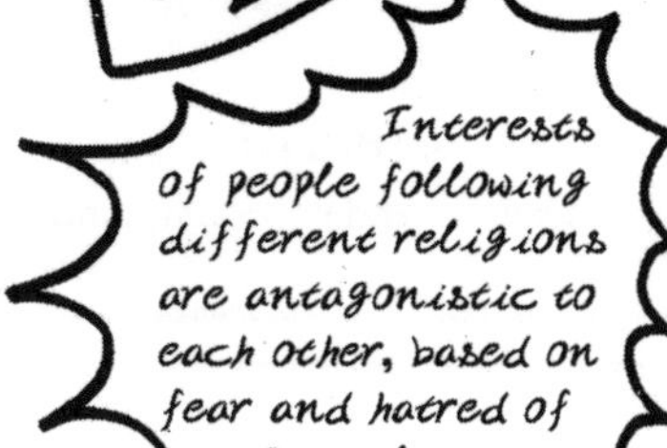

Slow pace of transition from a feudal structure to a modern set up results in consolidation of religion/ caste based identities.
In a limited job market, competition based on religion/ caste communal politics is handy to (a) hide economic frustrations, (b) hide the real source of miseries and (c) Mask the relationship between exploiter and the exploited.

Sometimes religious/caste distinctions coincide with economic distinctions. e.g., the exploiting sections (landlord, moneylender and merchant) were upper-caste Hindu and the exploited are poor peasant, landless labour, etc, were low-caste or Muslims

"Basis of Politics"

Feudal structure (kingdoms)	**Colonial/Modern society**
Favour/Reward succession	**Mobilization competition**

Common Features
Hindu Communalism- Muslim Communalism

Came from declining sections of society, landlords and kings
No struggle against British: Subtly encouraged by British
Congress denigrated and despised
Supported by elites of the communities only
Believed that Hindus and Muslims are separate nations
Mutual hatred for each other
Strengthened each other.
Spread fear against each other
Believed in hierarchy of caste and gender: Feudal value system
Opposed to democratic values
Their politics consolidated the colonialists
Even currently they are on the side of US imperialists policies

Nehru and Bhagat Singh-
Atheists and non-communal

Savarkar and Jinnah:
non-religious and communal

Gandhi & Abul Kalam Azad :
Deeply religious and
non-communal

MYTH
Kashmir is another example of Muslim Separatism
FACT
Let's have a look at the Kashmir issue.
At the time of independence, there were over six hundred princely states.
1947
These states were given three options,
A) TO MERGE WITH INDIA,
B) TO MERGE WITH PAKISTAN,
C) TO REMAIN INDEPENDENT
The kings were given the guidelines to take a decision based on physical proximity and the opinion of people. While problem of most of the states was solved with ease, the Kings of Hyderabad, Junagarh and Kashmir showed a bit of a hesitation in taking decision.
Hyderabad and Junagarh were merged into India by military action.

Jammu and Kashmir was a Muslim majority state with over 80% Muslims.
Kashmir's King Hari Singh wanted to remain independent and he had the vision of developing Kashmir into Switzerland of Asia . . .
Before any conclusive decision could be reached about the status of Kashmir, Pakistan invaded Kashmir through the army disguised as tribals.
Maharaja Hari Singh left the valley for security reasons. Sheikh Abdullah the chief of National Conference played a major role in post aggression scenario. King began negotiations with India through emissaries for sending the army to Kashmir to defend Kashmir. Sheikh Abdullah backed it up and ensured that Indian army intervenes.
Nehru stated that unless some agreement is signed, India couldn't send its army to a state where it has no legal standing. Accordingly, a treaty of accession was drafted with the Article 370 for safeguarding the people of the state
ARTICLE 370

DO PRADHAN DO VIDHAN

Accession treaty's principle was 'Two Chiefs, Two Constitutions' (Do Pradhan Do Vidhan), India was to look after defence, external affairs, communication and currency while the assembly will decide all other matters.

By that time Pakistani army had already occupied 1/3rd of Kashmir.To avoid civilian casualties, ceasefire was declared and matter was taken to United Nations.

As per UN resolution, a plebiscite was to be held after both the armies vacated Kashmir. This could not take place so far. Pakistan declared its part of Kashmir as Azad Kashmir and Indian part had its Prime Minister and Sadar-e-Riyasat.

Indian Govt. came under pressure from the time Jana Sangh (the previous avatar of BJP) and other ultra national elements to forcibly merge Kashmir into India by diluting and gradually reducing the autonomy of Kashmir.

During this time the post of Kashmir's Prime minister was changed to Chief Minister and Sadar-e-Riyasat was changed over to Governor and gradually the reach of Indian constitution was extended to Kashmir. Indian Govt. started to supervise the affairs of Kashmir. Democratic process started getting weaker and weaker.

All the central governments had acted on the basis of disbelief in the local leadership. After the dismissal of Farouq Abdullah in 1984 and then the massive rigging of elections in 1987, the process of disillusion amongst the people in the valley was complete and the youth became more vulnerable to the path of violence. This initiated a process of alienation amongst Kashmiri youth.

This resulted in the rise of militancy due to the restrictions on the democratic process. The internal dissatisfaction started giving support to terrorism.

Taking advantage of this, Pakistan started sending its militants and the problem started getting worse by the day. Again Farouk Abdullah was jailed for seven long years, showing that the central Govt. did not trust the locally elected representatives.

Another factor was the Al Qaeda's entry. Al Qaeda, which had been set up by the US to fight against the Soviet army in Afghanistan, having achieved their goal there, a section of militants entered the valley.

The worsening communal scenario in India in the decade of 1980's, added fuel to the fire of terrorism in Kashmir. Meanwhile, communal angle was being given to the harmony prevalent between Kashmiri Pandits and the local Muslim population. Terrorists took advantage of that distortion. A section of terrorists did target the Hindus on purpose. A sense of fear and insecurity gripped the Hindus.

Jagmohan who was appointed the Governor of Kashmir, operated on the premise was that all Kashmiri Muslims are terrorists. And so if Pandits leave the valley he can firmly deal with the militants. Accordingly, he offered to Pandits the transport to leave the valley. The local leaders of Muslim community opposed the move to the hilt. But encouraged by Jagmohan, the Pandits left the valley and are living the wretched life in refugee camps.

It also must be noted that in the victims of terrorist violence there are large number of Muslims also who either were killed or had to leave the valley.

Essentially a problem between two neighbouring countries has been given a communal colour. Kashmiri leadership had all the opportunity to merge with Pakistan but they did not do so all through. And even today many a Kashmiri Muslims are opposed to a merger with Pakistan.

Despite the severe alienation resulting due to the policies of Indian rulers, the suppression of their ethnic aspirations and due to repeated dismissal of popular govt. by the Indian Govt., the Kashmiri people even today are not opting for Pakistan as the alternative.

Their main demand has been to preserve their autonomy as promised in the treaty of accession; their main aspiration is to preserve the ethnic character of Kashmir and to be able to live the life away from the crossfire resulting due to the interference of Pakistan and mistrust of the Indian state. One of the recent opinion polls conducted by Outlook (Oct. 16, 2000) reveals that according to 74% of the respondents separate identity of Kashmir is what is required, 16% favoured greater autonomy and only 2% wanted merger with Pakistan. 39% still felt that a solution could be found within the framework of Indian constitution.

The major spurt in the activities of Militants took place from 1990 onwards, in the aftermath of the rigged elections of 1987.
We will have a look at some of the figures of the casualties and destruction of property in Kashmir by the militants.

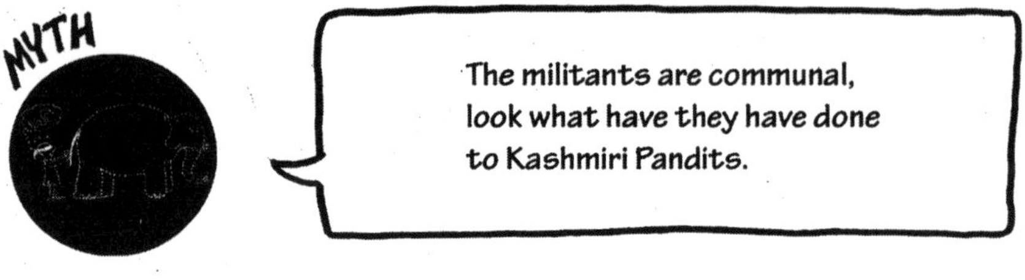

The large scale migration of Pandits from the valley is a big blow to the traditions of the valley. As the figures above show the damage by militants is to both the communities and not to Hindus alone. The Pandits had considered migration first in 1986 but this decision was held in abeyance due to the appeals of a goodwill mission, which was constituted by reputed Kashmiris, steeped in plural culture.

In 1990 the militancy was stepped up.

This time around Mr. Jagmohan, the hardcore right winger was the *Governor* of Kashmir and he ensured dissolution of the goodwill mission to Pandits by pressurizing one of the Pandit members of the team to migrate to Jammu. Balraj Puri in March 1990 stated "I found no hostility among common Muslims in Kashmir against Pandits, and that allegations of gross violations of human rights by security forces needs to be investigated" (Puri, 66).

At that time Hindu communal forces took it upon themselves to spread fear and terror amongst Pandits, "Much disinformation is being spread in Jammu and Delhi that scores of Hindu temples and the shrines have been desecrated or destroyed in Kashmir. This was only partly true and it is baffling that the *Government* has not thought it fit to ask Doordarshan to do a program on mandirs in Kashmir just to reassure people that they remain unharmed." (Press Council of India, 1991)

Thus the problem of Pandits' migration is an unfortunate outcome of the alienation of Kashmiri people resulting in militancy, Hindu communalist outfits' baseless spreading of fear psychosis and pressure of Governor Jagmohan and not due to the Hindu-Muslim hostility.

India is supposed to be religious country above everything else... [And yet] I have frequently condemned (religion) and wished to make a clean sweep of it. Almost always it seemed to stand for blind belief and reaction, dogma and bigotry, superstition and exploitation. And yet I know well that there was something else in, it, and something that supplied a deeper inner craving of human being.

-Nehru

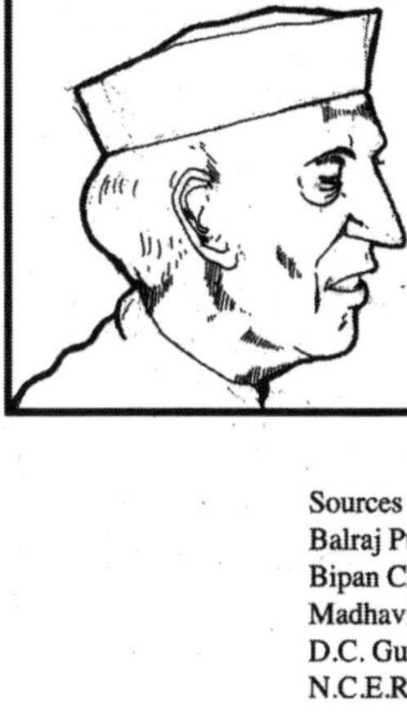

Religion and state will be separate. I swear by my religion. I will die for it. But it is my personal affair. The state has nothing to do with it. The state will look after your secular, welfare, health, communication, foreign relations, currency and so on, but not your or my religion.

That is everybody's personal concern.

-Gandhi

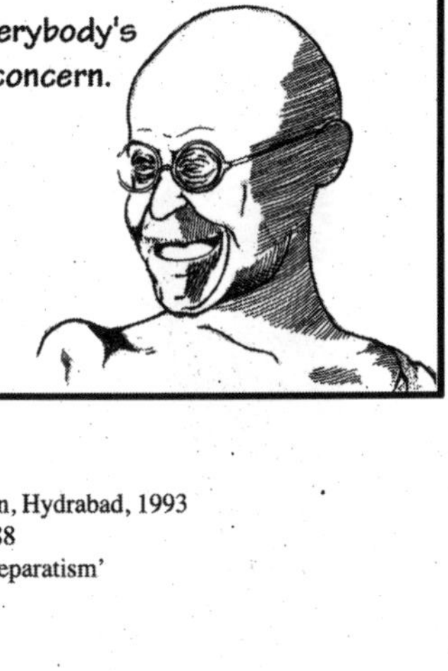

Sources -
Balraj Puri: 'Kashmir Towards Insurgency', Orient Longman, Hydrabad, 1993
Bipan Chandra: 'India's Struggle for Freedom', Penguin 1988
Madhavi Yasin, 'Emergence of Nationalism Congress and Separatism'
D.C. Gupta: 'Indian Nationalist Movement', Vikas, 1970
N.C.E.R.T. 'India's Struggle for Independence' 1997

MUSLIM COMMUNAL POLITICS

The events that started unfolding from 11th September, leading to the attack on World Trade Centre (WTC) loss of around three thousand lives, have been most tragic to say the least. The tragedy was too immense. Any condemnation of the terrorists is too less. American establishment immediately sprung to action, it declared Osama Bin Laden as the culprit and asked Afghanistan's Taliban to hand him over. Taliban wanted the proof of Osama's involvement and in case proved offered to hand him over in a neutral country.

US decided to attack Afghanistan.

Interestingly we have become used to the words Islamic terrorists. Islamic terrorism has become a much-used word, being synonym to culprit of most of the problems in the world.

The tragic Afghan war saw the usual miseries, the victims being the ordinary people of Afghanistan, while Osama hid like a pin in some haystack, and till date could not be caught.

Some of the sections of Muslim community identified with Osama, most of the Muslim rulers scattered all over the world sided with US in its attack on Afghanistan. While a section of Muslim community tried to project that this is the war on Islam, most of the moderate elements amongst Muslims condemned the attack on WTC and the terrorism, which has caused this.

Surprisingly the media highlighted the rabid section amongst the Muslim community and ignored the sane pleas and statements of liberal Muslim voice.

Close at home Islamic Fundamentalism has played its nasty role in Pre-Independence time when Muslim League put forward the idea of separate nation for the followers of Islam. This party of Jinnah never got more than six percent of votes in elections. Propped up by British and supported in his two Nation theory by Hindu fundamentalists, Pakistan was formed and the tragedy of Partition took place. During partition, a section of affluent Muslims left for Pakistan but majority of Muslims in this region remained here only. The same Pakistan, which was formed on the basis of religion, broke later (1971) into Pakistan and Bangladesh, proving that Nations cannot be formed on the basis of religion. Muslim fundamentalism did persist here in pockets and surfaced time and over again to give provocation to the Majority fundamentalism. Also the rulers here kept propping up the fundamentalist sections of Muslims.

Islam can be the basis of Nation state!

No modern Nation state can survive on the basis of religion. If we see we can make out that Muslim countries had also good deal of fights with each other, Iran-Iraq being the foremost.

Also the break up of Pakistan proved that religion couldn't be the binding factor. While the citizenship based on democratic principles is the only bond, which can put together in a single bond.

Islam is not the only religion in which fundamentalism has developed in History. The first major fundamentalist streak was seen in the Christian religion in the late 19th century in United States. This came in the backdrop of changing social situation due to abolition of slavery and due to women entering the social space in a big way.

Later Ayatollah Khomeini's Iran saw the rise of Fundamentalism. The policies of Raza Shah Pehlvi, who was a puppet of US, had a lot to do with this. He concentrated on superficial westernization at the cost of social development, resulting in rise in social misery leading to rebellion. Since there was no other strong pole giving the expression to social dissatisfaction, Ayatollah Khomeini could "succeed" in bringing in the fundamentalist regime.

BEFORE 1947

Many people believe that all followers of Islam form an Ummah (Islamic fraternity). But Ummah cannot be equated to the Global Islamic state. It is neither feasible nor practicable to believe in this. People can have International communities; rather all of us should constitute a World community based on Humanism.

AFTER 1947

But the existence and persistence of nation states is a reality at political level and it cannot be translated into a World following one or the other religion. We have witnessed the fights between different Islamic states. The experiment of Arab nationalism, different Arab Muslim nations coming together to form a Nation was a miserable failure. We have also witnessed the break up of Pakistan, despite the fact that the components, East and West Pakistan had same religion. We have witnessed strife between neighbouring Islamic countries, Iran-Iraq, Iraq- Kuwait etc.

The Ulemas represent the Muslims

Many a Shahi Imams and other Ulemas often claim that they are speaking for their religion and so are representatives of Muslim community. The interpretation of Islam keeps varying depending on the socio-political circumstances. Any religious, holy people cannot do the representation of communities. In India especially from 1970s many a politicians have tried to groom the section of Ulemas for their political benefit. Janata party's (1977) representatives V.P. Singh and Atal Bihari Vajpayee approached Shahi Imam of Jama Masjid of Delhi to issue a fatwa in support of their party. Similarly many other politicians have played this game times and over again. Ulema are not the representatives of community. Only elected people can represent the communities.

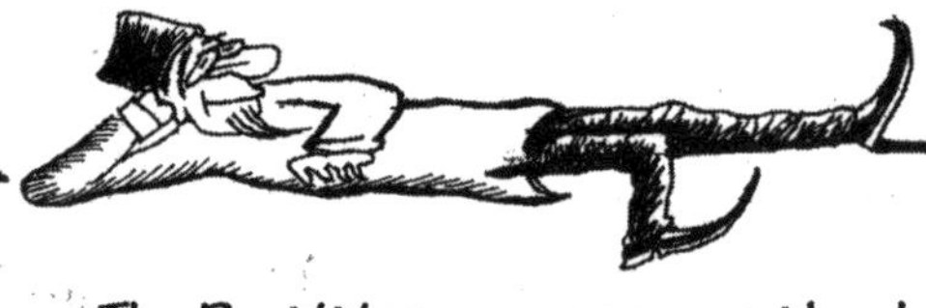

The Partition process was the demand of Muslims and acted in their benefit

We have seen above that this process was led by the elite of Muslim community, the landlord and the salariat (top bureaucrats) class. The average Muslim did not support this politics and was more for the composite Indian Nationalism. At the best of times Muslim League did not get more than 6 per cent of votes.

The major leaders of Muslim community like Maulana Abul Kalam Azad, Khan Abdul Gaffar Khan and also the Ulemas of Barelvi and Deoband school stood for composite Indian nationalism.

The Pakistan resolution was opposed by the poor Muslims, artisans etc as being detrimental to the interests of poor Muslims.

But due to British encouragement and due to the religious hysteria created by Muslim League, the Partition of India had to be conceded.

Shah Bano Movement was for the benefit of Muslim community.

Shah Bano judgment was a legal issue in which the court had granted maintenance to the divorcee. The fundamentalist elements amongst the community raised hue and cry and the government brought legislation in the parliament to reverse the same.

It was unfortunate that the government to gain short-term benefits appeased the fundamentalist section of society. The government consistently appeased this section while putting the needs of Muslim masses on the backburner. As we have seen the Muslim community shares its problems with the other poor and deprived of the society and political opportunism has appeased fundamentalists of both the communities. Like the Shah Bano episode was 'balanced' by the opening of the locks of Babri Mosque. Here also the government capitulated to the fundamentalists of another community.

Fundamentalist politics stands for the status quo. It is opposed to the social transformation towards caste and gender equality. It does not benefit the poor of the community and is imposed in the name of religion. The rulers, as a shortcut many a times appease the fundamentalists of the community at the cost of interest of average and deprived people of society.

MYTH

Islam gives rise to terrorism

FACT

It is in very recent memory that to suit its ambitions and goals US had propped up Taliban to fight against Russian occupation of Afghanistan, it also armed Iraq against Iran in the war between the two countries. And ironically later it turned against first Iraq and paralyzed it by an attack, and now it is planning to 'teach a lesson to Taliban'.

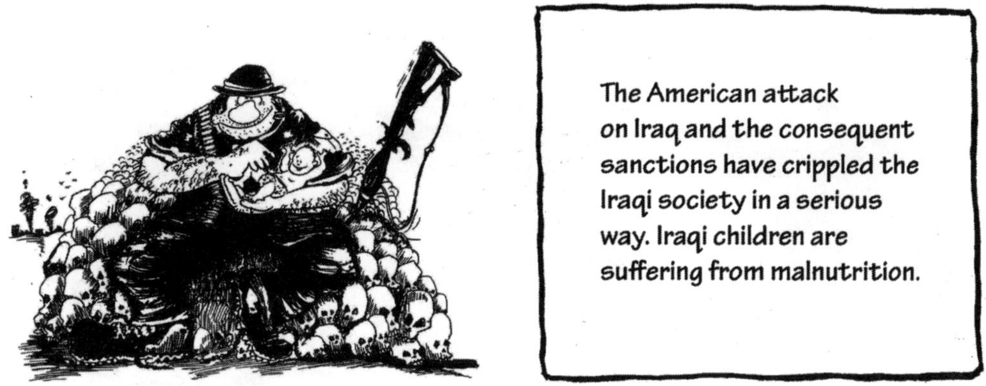

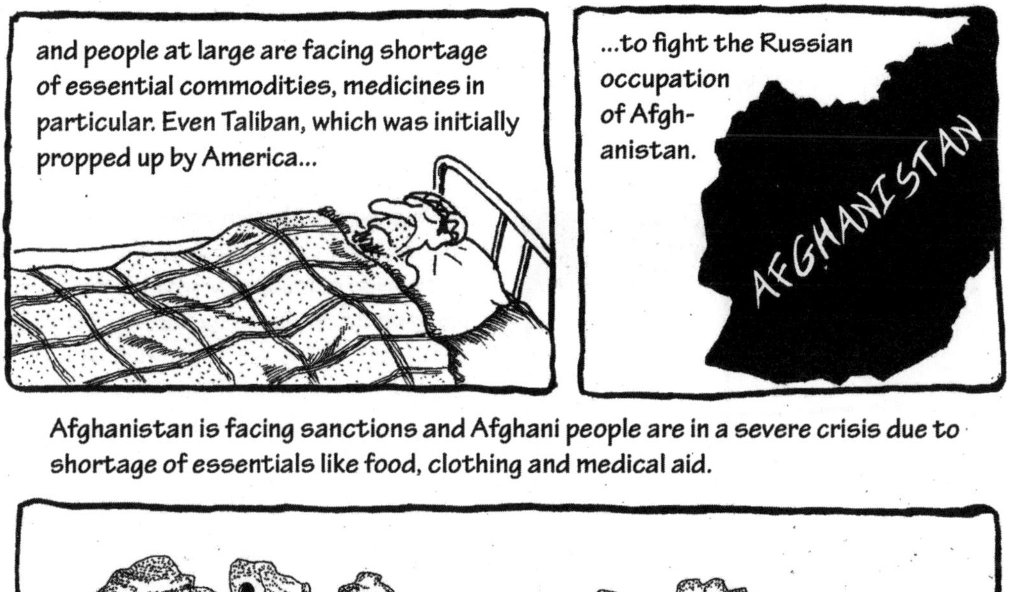

Afghanistan is facing sanctions and Afghani people are in a severe crisis due to shortage of essentials like food, clothing and medical aid.

The tale of Palestinians merits a severe introspection about the ways of the superpowers. It also gives insight to the 'rise' of militancy amongst particular ethnic groups. Jews, needed world sympathy due to the atrocities of Hitler's race based Nationalism, but they also had to be restrained when they themselves started practicing blatant racism against the native Palestinian people.

Israel kept being supported against the Palestinians on various flimsy grounds unmindful of the aspirations and human rights of Palestinians.

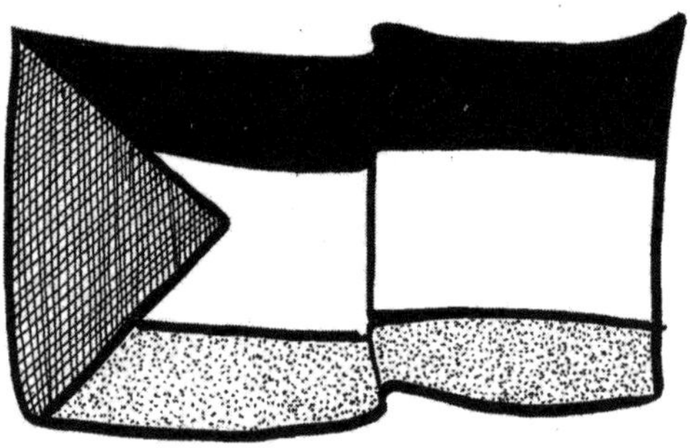

The highhanded Israeli actions, condoned by the superpowers led to the rise of militancy, which defied being controlled even by the supercops of the world. It is not that Muslims are the only victims of lopsided policies going against them in different parts of the world.

Down south, Sinhala highhandedness did lead to the rise of Tamil (Hindu) militancy and just a decade ago Indian state put all its might to finish Sikh militancy coming in the form of demand for separate Khalistan. Different ethic groups faced with diverse forms of repression and injustices have resorted to these inhuman responses to the repression of their rights.

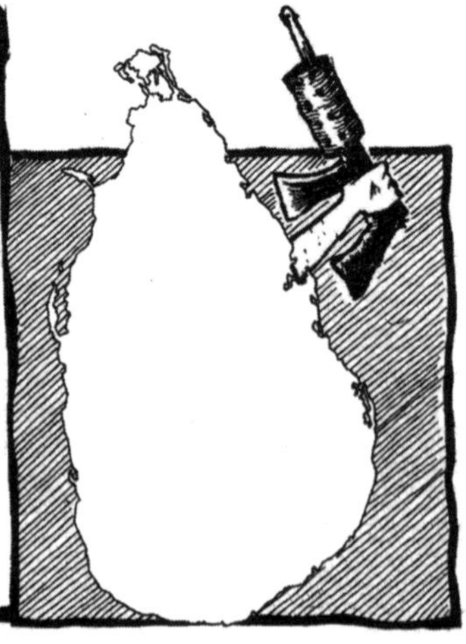

With the collapse of Socialist Russia the balance of power at global level has suffered an irretrievable set-back. In this post "collapse of socialist states" scenario, America has been behaving as a global supercop, ignoring the role of United Nations (UN) and many a times even forcing UN to toe its line by different bullying tactics.

And as imperialism always needs an 'external enemy' to maintain its military complex, Islam and Islamic fundamentalism was given this place by Uncle Sam. Islam has not only been demonized but also projected as the major threat to the world freedom.

It is during this phase that miseries of Palestine, Iraq, Bosnia, Rwanda and Afghanistan came to the fore. US reduced UN's role to a helpless observer of the acts of commission by US.

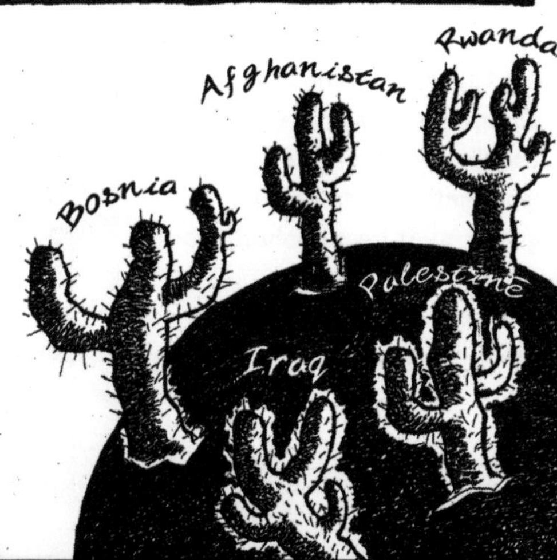

Surely the present dastardly act of terrorists is a sad reminder that even disadvantaged groups, who are nowhere equal to the might of the most powerful nation, can occasionally puncture the high handedness of bullies.

Whatever be the slogan under which both these operate we have to strive for a just and humane society. In the charged atmosphere created due to the inhuman acts of terrorists, it is likely and one fears that particular group of people to which the terrorists belong may be hounded and intimidated for no fault of theirs. Terrorists do not represent any community. They are a cancerous growth on the body of society. Today world as a whole needs to introspect about the seeds of discontent, which have been giving rise to terrorists. It will be easy enough for American might to destroy a country or two in the act of retaliation but that will not give us back the precious lives lost during a period of couple of hours of terror by the disgruntled elements.

Punishing the innocent individuals belonging to one or the other religion to which the terrorists belong will hardly solve the problem. The mass sentiments against particular community may cause uncalled for violence against innocent individuals. The guilty must be punished but innocents have to be protected from the wrath of mass hysteria.

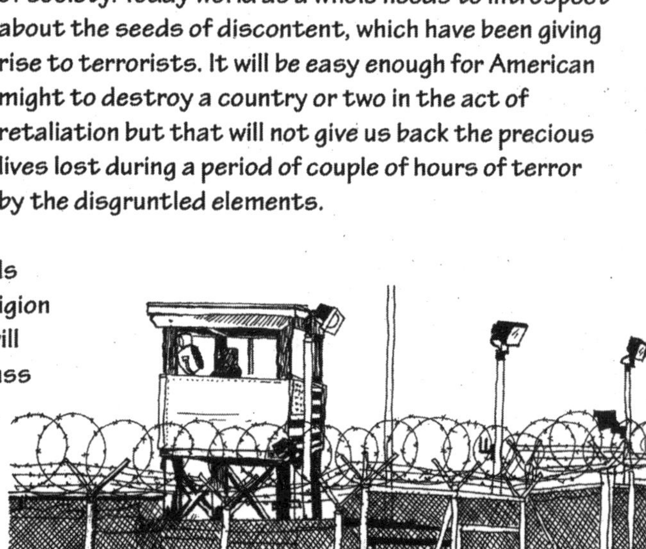

These understandings have serious flaws, as they do not look beyond the nose of those promoting these ideas. How is Islam related to terror, or for that matter how is any religion related to the cult of violence?

Were the crusades undertaken by Christian kings to promote Christianity? Did Muslim kings undertaken Jihad to promote Islam? Were the Dharmayudhas by Hindu kings undertaken to promote Hindu religion? By no stretch of imagination any war related violence could be attributed to these religions. It is the kings whose basic goal was to expand their kingdoms, who undertook these wars and misused the names of their religions to get more people involved in the same.

Timothy McViehg, Oklahoma bomber was not serving Christianity, neither Dhanu was serving Hinduism when she acted as a live bomb killing Rajiv Gandhi and innocents around him, nor was Bhindranwale serving Sikhism when he promoted the cult of violence which led to murder of Indira Gandhi and then the butchery of thousands of Sikhs, nor was Osama bin-Laden serving Islam when he thanked Allah in the wake of the WTC tragedy, nor are the Kashmiri militants serving Islam when they maim and kill innocent Hindus and Muslims in Kashmir.

Terrorism is the product of social and National discontent, discontent, which flows through the barrel of the gun or explodes with the bomb of terrorist when the democratic channels are not available for its expression for the victims of injustice. People belonging practically to all the religions under the sun have resorted to terror in the name of their religions. It is not that only one religion has the distinction for this misuse.

In Indian context the terrorism of Khalistanis could be contained when the dealing with the militants could be combined with winning over the hearts and minds of people and by making available the effective democratic options to the people at large. The present terrorism by the self proclaimed Jihadis is definitely a slightly different ball game. The role of Pakistan in this is very discernible. But here our myopic vision stops and fails to see the imperialist designs in promoting the terrorism and routing this through the conduit of Pakistan. We are unable to see the deeper imperialist goals of control over oil resources, which has nurtured Talibans.

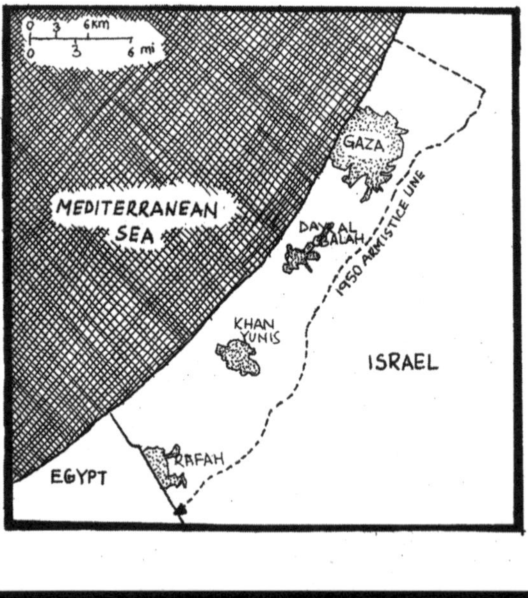

Right since the formation of Israel and its being backed by US the signals were around of its designs in the Middle East and then in the subcontinent. Israel went into violate all the UN resolutions, attack Arab world repeatedly, to capture the Palestinian lands and to cause the loss of home and hearth of close to a million Palestinians.

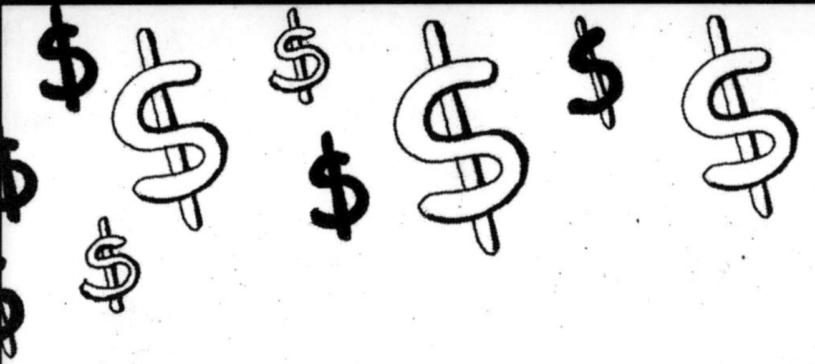

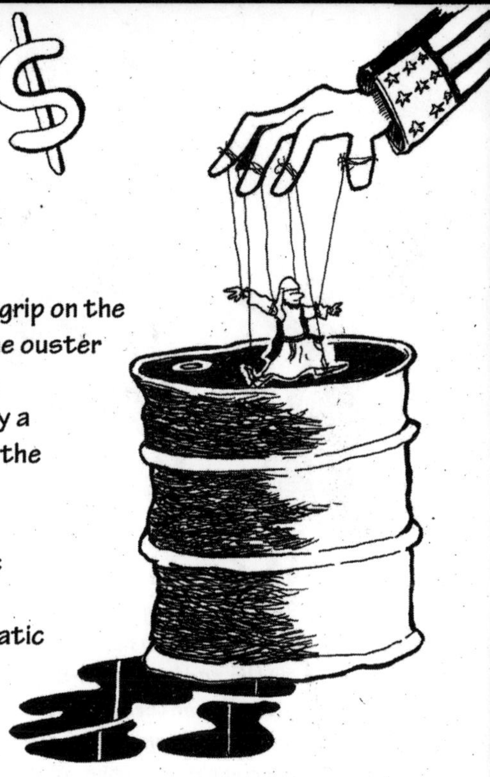

In due course US started tightening its grip on the resources of the region. First it helped in the ouster of Mossadegh (Iran), who was planning to nationalize its oil wells and replacing that by a puppet Raza Shah Pehlavi regime to ensure the cheap flow of oil.

Later it went all out to promote the fanatic groups in Afghanistan to fight the Russian occupation. Since then the base for the fanatic camps was laid in the region.

Pakistan as the handmaiden of US imperialism kept acting as the conduit to promote the US interests by all possible means. US to keep its hegemony in the region was playing different games. With Ayatullah Khoemeni replacing the US stooge Raza Shah Pehlavi; US backed Iraq, in Iran-Iraq war for many years. Later it turned its barrel against Iraq itself on the pretext of rescuing the Sheikh of Kuwait and his sovereignty.

With the Russian occupation being pushed back the fanatics, basically products of US training, started intruding into Kashmir, in the process worsening the Kashmir imbroglio, where due to weak democratic institutions the alienation of Kashmiri people acted as the base for the terrorist game and the green valley turned red with the bullets flowing from the barrels of militants and the Indian army.

The dissatisfaction in the Arab world initially got manifested through the terrorist attacks on Jews. The terrorism here had two dimensions, one anti-Israel-US and later anti-Soviet occupation. US encouraged the latter through the conduit of ISI. Now after 9/11 the cycle has turned full circle giving further pretext to US to interfere more in the affairs of the region. The end of Socialist block has also marked the beginning of the demise of the role and power of UN, whatever it was worth. With US acting as the super cop and super bully rolled into one the problems do not seem to have their respite. So contrary to US's own attitude vis a vis 9/11, a blind reprisal and aggression on the Afghanistan, it is advising restraint to India on one hand and increasing its own grip in the region on the other.

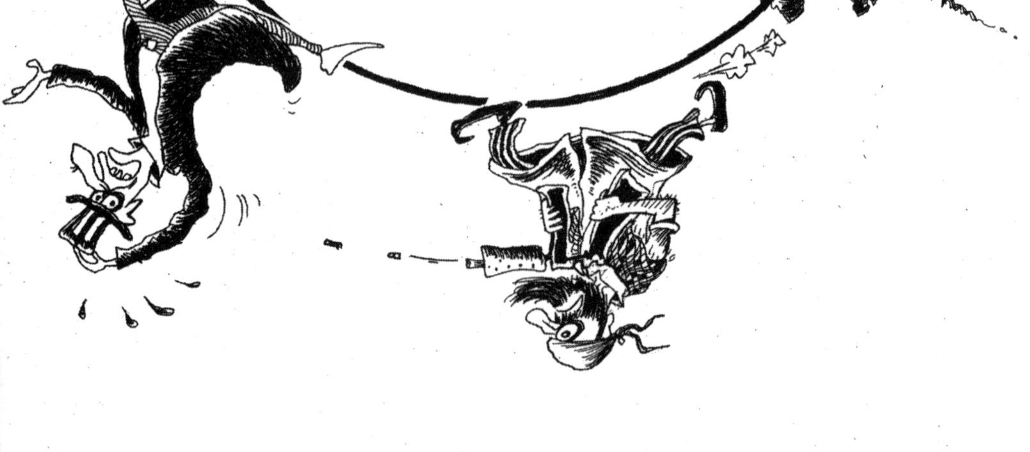

So who is responsible for the genesis of terrorism? Is it a religious phenomenon? Is it due to the members of a single community? How come some people come to take the steps, which surely are suicidal for them? Terrorism is basically a political phenomenon. People belonging to different religious communities have resorted to it. The prerequisite of this is of course an intense injustice perpetrated by the dominant group. Be it Israel, or Sinhala ethnic politics or the sense of alienation felt by the people like in Kashmir or North East.

The sustaining factor for this phenomenon is the abuse of democratic norms. It's an act of extreme desperation where the victims do not see any light at the end of the tunnel. Comparing the miseries of Kashmiri Pandits and the victims of communal carnage will not be fair. Both are sipping their own cups of woes and these are not of the same quality or quantity. The three major points due to which Islam and Muslims are demonized are scattered all over. The problem of Palestine is the major one. It is a mere coincidence that the regions, which are rich in oil wealth, also happen to be the regions where followers of Islam are more. These are also the areas where American Imperialism wants to control the oil wealth and prop up despotic rulers in these countries who have nothing whatsoever to do with democracy.

The issue of Kashmir has been a matter of great anguish for the Kashmiri people. The initial policies due to which the dictum of Do Pradhan Do Vidhan (Two Prime Ministers-Two Constitutions) was violated resulted in the alienation of large sections of Kashmiri youth, making them fertile ground for terrorist ideas and actions.

The rise of Hindutva, the communal violence, has again resulted in the violence in which Minorities are the big victims. The lack of justice mechanism, the failure to implement the inquiry committee reports and the communalization of civic society has given a deep sense of hurt to the Muslim minorities. The demonization of minorities is by now complete due to the continuous efforts of RSS and its progeny. The doctoring of mass consciousness has gone to the extent that average person has come to believe that Islam is the religion, which promotes violence, and that Muslims are devils incarnate.

In a way Islam worldwide is demonized in pursuit of the Imperialist ambitions of US, more so after the demise of Soviet Union, Islam has been projected to be the backward religion. This has been backed up by the ideologues of Imperialism like Samuel Huntington who see the present obstacles to America's ambitions to control the world's oil wealth as a clash between the advanced Western civilization and the backward Islamic civilization. Can any civilization be totally dictated by religion at any point of time, more so in the current times?

What is the similarity between the civilization of an Islamic country like Indonesia and Saudi Arabia? What is common between the Muslim population of Japan or US and the believers in the cult of Osama bin Laden?

Kashmir is another sore point but it is hardly an issue related to Islam or for that matter to the Indian Muslims. Hindutva surely has made great 'strides' and the original proclamation of the RSS Sarsanghchalak that Muslims and Christians don't deserve even the citizen's rights is being implemented by the saffron eyed boy of Sangh Parivar, Narendra Modi, with great admiration from the top rulers of the country as a whole.

So what is primary-does terrorism give rise to Israel-US policies or do US-Israel atrocities result in Osama bin Laden and his clan? Has Kashmir terrorism its roots in Islam or in the unresolved Indo-Pakistani relations and using the people of Kashmir as the hostages to two supra-nationalisms, that of Pakistan and India?

Does terrorism give rise to Gujarat carnage or Gujarat carnage gives rise to Gujarat Muslim Revenge group, which causes Mumbai blasts? In this case they are an interesting twist. Mr. Modi will like us to believe that Godhra terrorism gave rise to Gujarat carnage. A deeper analysis will show that Godhra was projected as a terrorist offense to legitimize in advance the carnage which was planned much before. The Hindutva and for that matter all narrow nationalism creates an enemy to ensure that their planned actions are projected as revenges to the original acts.

Madarsas are breeding ground for Terrorism

In recent years madarsas in India have come under increasing attack as being alleged 'dens of terror'. In particular, madarsas located on the border between India and Nepal have been decried as being reportedly associated with the Pakistani Inter-Services' Intelligence.

Most of the madarsas are, indeed, conservative in their orientation and many of them are opposed to the inclusion of any modern disciplines in their curriculum. This, however, by no means suggests that they are 'anti-national'.The madarsas cater mainly to poor families. The vast majority of the Indian Muslims work as landless labourers, small or marginal peasants, artisans, petty shopkeepers and the like. More than half the urban Muslim population lives below the poverty line, and, as compared to Hindus, proportionately a considerably higher number of Muslims are self-employed. Given their structural location in the economy and the perception of discrimination, relatively few Muslims can afford or aspire to higher education.

A survey conducted in three districts of Uttar Pradesh that have a fairly high Muslim population, characterized by high rates of illiteracy and widespread poverty: Siddharthnagar, Barabanki and Moradabad, suggests that despite their obvious limitations, madarsas are playing a key role in promoting education among Muslims, especially those from poor families, and in areas where state educational provision is either non-existent or in a very bad shape. The survey discovered that although most parents are eager to provide quality education to their girl children they are unable to educate them due to economic conditions and the non-existant state school system rather then religion space. Muslim educational backwardness is largely a product of Muslim poverty and neglect by the state.

MUSLIM COMMUNALISM AND THE POLITICS OF FATWAS

ISLAMIC FATWAS AND CONTEMPERORARY SOCIETY

Lot is being heard about the fatwas on every issue possible, more so pertaining to women's lives, their dress code, their marital alliance and four marriages. The fatwas which made headlines for days pertained to the case of Gudiya, whose missing husband Arif, who was captured by Pakistani army while he was presumed to be a martyr in the battle, appeared on the scene when she was already pregnant from her second marriage.

The local panchayat, without asking her opinion ruled that she has to return to her first husband and after the child is born, she should hand it over to the second husband. In case of Imrana, whose father in law raped her, she was dictated to live with the rapist father-in-law and to abandon her husband. Her opinion was not sought.

This is what fatwa dictated. In another of such shameful fatwas an Arab was permitted to marry both the sisters in a single go, again under the umbrella of a fatwa. Marriages of girls under the age of 18 have also been solemnized under the cover of fatwa from some source.

Undoubtedly the fatwas have come to prominence and fore in last two decades in India more than before. While these are claimed to be the opinion of Islam, the fatwa (opinion) are different according to different schools of Islam, Shia and Sunni subsets are again different. The fatwa given on an issue in some part of India will be different from another part and surely it will be different in different countries. Theologically fatwa is just an opinion not binding in any legal or social terms.

It was a mechanism where thoughtful opinion was to be arrived at. With changing times the nature and import of fatwas has been changing. The most notorious one was against Salman Rushdie for his literary work which was regarded as derogatory to Mohammad Paigambar by Ayatollah Khomeini. In countries like Turkey, a predominantly Muslim country, the fatwas were dumped in the backyard and secular rules preferred.

Fatwas have generally been delivered by the bearded Maulanas, residing in this or that Islamic seminary, cut off from the social milieu of the community. Most of the fatwas are very derogatory to the women. According to some liberal Islamic opinions they are not having any validity as another set of Alims (learned men) will interpret the same issue in a different light.

The real issue is that when a community feels threatened and intimidated it falls more and more in the grip of these conservative elements, which have their own vested interests to grind. In India one can clearly see that with the rise of anti-Muslim violence the retrograde fatwas are being dished out more in frequency, there is a strong effort to impose it on the society and they are given more prominence.

The same fatwas are used by the dominant communal elements to further demonize Islam and the Muslims. The healthy trend is that a large section of liberal Muslims who was earlier keeping quiet in the face of fatwas, is now taking a strong and clear cut stand against the self proclaimed custodians of Islam, the Maulavis and Malians. More number of Muslim women themselves are standing firm to oppose these fatwas. The battle for gender justice and humane values requires internal reforms combined with provision of security for the community to reduce the vice like grip of fatwa delivering Maulanas.

Even in self-proclaimed Islamic states today there is a clearly defined legal bar on the minimum age for marriage. The ulema, however, inhabit a world of their own. At its national meet in Hyderabad in late 2002, the All India Muslim Personal Law Board (AIMPLB) had demanded that Muslims be exempted from the provisions of the Child Marriage Restraint Act, 1929.

There are efforts to make 'shariat' courts as a parallel judicial system in the country.

The fact that the protests from within the community could not overrule these fatwas is a cause of great concern. The community as well as the civil society has to realize that this is the first step towards talibanisation and this has to be resisted strongly.

(Courtesy Anhad, In Defense of Our Dreams, Shabnam Hashmi)

Hindu Mahasabha and R.S.S: Growth and Role in Freedom Struggle

Veer Savarkar has been one of the greatest revolutionaries who fought for India's freedom

This needs to be questioned seriously. We see that Savarkar was involved in militant anti-British struggles till his imprisonment.

From 1923 Hindu Mahasabha's politics was guided by Savarkar. As pointed out above, he contributed to this politics by his activities and ideological contributions. Prior to this in England Savarkar had formed 'Free Indian Society' committed to overthrowing British rule in India.

At that time he had gone to study law, in London and for his anti-British stance he was denied the barrister-ship. He rejected the British proposal to give the undertaking not to participate in politics.

One member of the group killed a top ranking official in India office (London)for which he was sentenced to death. Savarkar for his association with the assassin and for another charge on him in Indian courts was arrested and was to undergo life imprisonment. He was deported from England. The ship carrying him stopped at Marseilles, where he jumped into the sea and swam to the shore to claim asylum on French soil.

He was captured and was transported to Andamans for life imprisonment. The conditions of jail life broke his spirits. From 1920 INC was asking for his unconditional release, but due to reasons best known to him, Savarkar preferred to give a written undertaking, which in a way was the total surrender.

'I hereby acknowledge that I had a fair trial and just sentence. I heartily abhor methods of violence resorted to in days gone by and I feel myself duty bound to uphold law and constitution (British, added) to the best of my powers and am willing to make the reform a success in so far as I may be allowed to do so in future' (from facsimile of Savarkar's letter to British authorities, Frontline, April 7, 1995. Pg.94), the reforms he is referring to here is the Montague Chelmsford proposals of 1919 which did not satisfy the nationalist movement's demands.

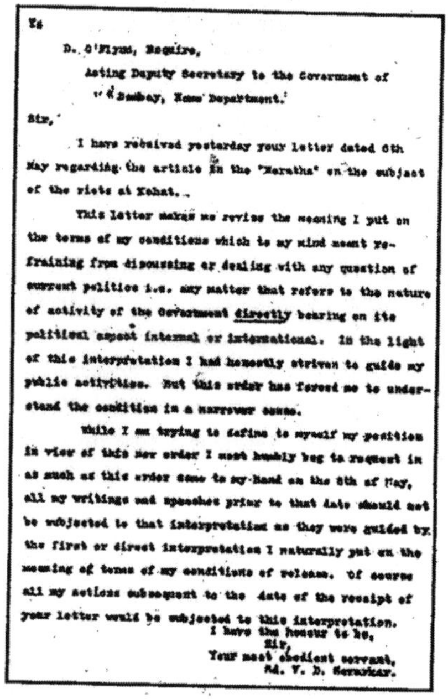

To

D. O'Flynn, Esquire,

Acting Deputy Secretary to the Government of Bombay, Home Department.

Sir,

I have received yesterday your letter dated 6th May regarding the article in the "Maratha" on the subject of the riots at Kohat.

This letter makes me revise the meaning I put on the terms of my conditions which to my mind meant refraining from discussing or dealing with any question of current politics i.e. any matter that refers to the nature of activity of the Government directly bearing on its political aspect internal or international. In the light of this interpretation I had honestly striven to guide my public activities. But this order has forced me to understand the condition in a narrower sense.

While I am trying to define to myself my position in view of this new order I most humbly beg to request in as much as this order came to my hand on the 8th of May, all my writings and speeches prior to that date should not be subjected to that interpretation as they were guided by the first or direct interpretation I naturally put on the meaning of terms of my conditions of release. Of course all my actions subsequent to the date of the receipt of your letter would be subjected to this interpretation.

I have the honour to be,
Sir,
Your most obedient servant,
Sd. V. D. Savarkar.

In response to this, as a trade off, the British Government released him under the condition that he will stay in the Ratnagiri district in Bombay province and will seek permission of the government to leave the district. Also that he will not engage in any public or private political activities without the consent of the government.

The period of conditions lasted till 1937, when the Congress ministry was sworn in and subsequent to this he assumed the office of the President of Hindu Mahasabha.

This aspect of his total surrender is completely hidden by the Hindutva forces, they confer on him the epithet of "Veer (brave) Savarkar". Why did British government release him ? How is it that after his release the thrust of his politics totally changed and he came to adorn the mantle of ideologue of Hindu Rashtra? How is it that later he never undertook any anti British agitation? How is it that he never joined and supported the major movements of those times like Quit India movement? How is it that instead of being a part of freedom struggle, he chose to help the British in recruiting Indians for their army? One can have one's own inferences. But he did emerge as the undisputed leader of Hindu Mahasabha. The calculations of British in releasing him stood vindicated by his pro-British and anti-Gandhi stance, and he became the willing accomplice of the divide and rule policy of British colonialists. Dube and Ramkrishanan (Frontline - ibid) have this to say "Is it possible that the British Government was using Savarkar to create an anti Congress outfit, discovering in him Hindu Jinnah, to help them effectively implement their 'divide-and-rule' policy ?"

Post-1937, his politics was the polar opposite of National movement led by Gandhi and "no support to Congress" was his basic dictum. This can be best exemplified in the 1942 Quit India movement, when Gandhi gave the call for the people to leave the government, but Savarkar issued the edict "I issue this definite instruction to all Hindu Sanghathanists in general holding any post or position of vantage in the government services, should stick to them and continue to perform their regular duties". (Quoted in A G Noorani, Frontline, Dec.1,1995).

Also the Congress Working Committee(CWC) had passed a resolution on August 31, 1942 asking all Mahasabhaites to remain at their jobs. After Gandhi's murder he was also one of the accused, but was let off for the lack of sufficient evidence. This is sufficient to tell us that his revolutionary career was short lived and later all his energies were directed in 'opposing' the movement for freedom struggle.

Hindutva is newer term for Hinduism and is 'our' way of life

This is far from true. Hinduism has many religious streams like Tantra, Bhakti, Kabir, Tukaram, Shaiva, Vaishanav etc. From the beginning of 19th century only Brahminism is being projected and asserted as Hinduism. Hindutva is a brew of Brahminical Hinduism with Nationalism. Savarkar is the major ideologue of Hindutva. He spelt his ideas in his book, "Who is a Hindu?" As per him Hindu is one who regards this land spread from Sindhu to the seas as his fatherland and holy land.

So patriotism of all 'non-Hindus' whose holy land is not in India, is inferior in status. He asserts that Hindutva means reverence for common culture and common civilization. Hindutva projected Ram as a symbol of national identity.

COMPARING THE CONCEPT OF HINDUISM AND HINDUTVA

HINDUISM	HINDUTVA
A collation of multiple traditions Brahminism-Shramanism-Tantra, Kabir, Tukaram, Nanak	Politics of Hindu elite, drawing from Brahminical Hinduism. Began as the politics of Rajas (Kings) and Zamindars (landlords)
Brahminism is based on ethos of Caste system Brahminism was projected as THE Hinduism initially in 6th - 10th century, then in early 19th century, Brahminical Hinduism was projected to be synonymous with Hinduism.	Brew of Brahminical Hinduism and Nationalism Aims at Hindu Rashtra based on Brahminical Hinduism
Shramanic traditions: There were constant rebellions and attempts to escape the clutches of Brahminism, including conversion to Buddhism (early times and now after the lead given by Ambedkar).	Led initially by Brahmins and Banias: Even now dominant leadership is from upper castes.
'Dharma' is caste based religious duties.	Political expression through Sangh Parivar now, earlier Hindu Mahasabha and RSS.
Semitisation process being spear-headed by SP- Holy deity: Ram, Holybook: Gita, clergy: Shankaracharyas etc.	A mix of fundamentalism and fascism.
Its saint traditions are tolerant and Brahminical one's are intolerent.	VHP brought in the stink of fundamentalism in the essentially fascist politics of RSS, BJP and Bajrang Dal.

RSS was formed for building the Indian Nation.

The very formation of RSS was for building a Hindu Nation and not India. This was in contrast to the approach of INC and its foremost leader Mahatma Gandhi. Gandhi had a secular approach, mobilization of all sectors of society against British. This resulted in dissatisfaction of large number of Brahmins. In early 1920s, the failure of Khilafat movement, communal violence, Non-Brahmin (Phule-Ambedkar) in Maharashtra, idea of a Hindu organisation to promote interests of Hindus took shape. RSS was formed in 1925. It was an all male organisation based on principles of 'supreme dictator'. In Shakha Bauddhik's (intellectual training in RSS branches), a distorted version of history is instilled into young minds.

"Hindus alone constitute this nation as they are the original inhabitants of this land and have created this society and culture. Hinduism is very tolerant and catholic, which makes it superior to all other faiths, but this tolerance has been mistaken as weakness..... The Hindu nation has repeatedly been conquered by aliens, particularly the Muslims and then the Christian British.

Hindus must acquire strength through RSS to counter all the present and future threats. The subsequent entry and takeover by foreigners has created the illusion that India was the land of many different and equal cultures".

RSS formation was influenced and inspired by example of Nazis and Hitler. Its initial support came from rich landlords, traders and bureaucrats (Brahmins and Banias). RSS ideology projects Muslims as the main enemy of Hindus. It regarded Gandhi's goal of composite nationalism as futile. Its ideology glorifies past Hindu kings and mythification of history to communalise the society is its major activity. Golwalkar's writings give a fair idea of its ideology. Let's have a look at the quotes from "We or Our Nationhood Defined":

"Upholding national pride: To keep up the purity of nation and its culture, Germany shocked the world by her purging the country of the semitic races - the Jews. National pride at its highest has been manifested here. Germany has also shown how well-nigh impossible for races and cultures, having differences going to the root, to be assimilated into one united whole, a good lesson for us in Hindustan to learn and profit by."

Mahatma Gandhi after visiting the RSS camp on the request of RSS leadership and on a later occasion opined that 'it is a communal body with a totalitarian outlook'.

RSS Chief is Sarsanghchalak (supreme dictator), who is nominated for life, and nominates his successor, so far most of them have been Maharashtrian high caste Brahmins. It kept aloof from freedom struggle but was very visible in all activities around communal riots. It was nowhere around when the country was seriously engaged in anti –British struggles like: civil disobedience movement of 40-41, Quit India Movement of 1942, activities of Azad Hind Fauz, upsurges around INA trials and Bombay Naval mutiny. It never confronted British, and was not a target of British war time repression. Some people call it Rumour Spreading Society because of its expertise in effective use of rumours especially before and during communal riots.

Upholding racial pride...non-Hindu people in Hindustan must either adopt the Hindu culture and language, must entertain no idea but the glorification of Hindu nation i.e., they must not only give up their attitude of intolerance and ingratitude towards this land and its age-long traditions, but must also cultivate the positive attitude of love and devotion instead. In one word they must cease to be foreigners or may stay in this country wholly subordinated to the Hindu nation claiming nothing, deserving no privileges, far less any preferential treatment, not even citizens' rights.

M S Golwalkar, " We or Our Nationhood Defined" 1938, Nagpur

RSS has played a major role in our freedom struggle and "nation building"!

RSS did not play any role in freedom struggle, it denounced 'Quit India' movement and asked its followers to stick to its jobs during the period.

Nevertheless it claims to have contributed substantially in the process of nation building. The history text books introduced in schools wherever BJP governments have come to power delve at great length about the contribution of their ideologues in National movement claiming that Dr. Hedgewar was imprisoned during the freedom struggle. As a matter of fact Hedgewar joined the Satyagraha movement only briefly and was imprisoned for a short while, but overall the struggles leading to national independence are non-events for R.S.S.

Hedgewar dissociated himself from National movement from 1931 onwards from then on Dr. Hedgewar's ideological break up with the national movement was complete and he abstained from the freedom movement.

This non participation was ideologically formulated by M.S. Golwalkar, as per whom fighting against British is reactionary and he accused the Congress for reducing the national struggle to 'mere' anti British movement.

Golwalkar writes, "Being anti British was equated with patriotism and nationalism. This reactionary view had disastrous effect upon the entire course of the independence struggle, its leaders and the common people" (Golwalkar, 1966). Obviously, with this ideological formulation the Sangh Parivar did not and could not fight against the British. The RSS equated its nationalism with being against Muslims and hence its constant harp against the national leadership for 'appeasement of Muslims'.

The Hindu Mahasabha and RSS kept away even from Naval revolt because they (mutineers) used guns against the British and the RSS considered fighting against British as 'disastrous' and 'reactionary'. (Lala Lajpat Rai, Letter in Times of India, 18th Jan. 1994)

Anderson and Damle (Brotherhood in Saffron) point out 'Golwalkar believed that the British not be given any excuse to ban the RSS. On April 29, 1943 Golwalkar distributed a circular that 'We discontinue practice included in the governments order on military drill and uniforms to keep our work clearly within bounds of law, as every law abiding institution should ..." (Quoted in A G Noorani, Frontline, Dec. 1, 1995).

RSS in nutshell was not only consciously absent as far as freedom movement was concerned, it was acting from the opposite angle by opposing various movements (especially Quit India movement) and also by being active as a communal body. It played the role of boosting the impact of Muslim communalism and participating in the process of mutual supplementation of Hindu and Muslim communalism.

Atal Bihari Vajpayee participated in freedom struggle.

Much is also made of 'participation' of current BJP led coalition's Prime Minister, Mr. Atal Bihari Vajpayee (1998-99) in Quit India movement. This was the time when young Vajpayee was a recruit of RSS. In an article put on the net (this article also appeared in newspapers) 'The Sangh is my soul' for the consumption of NRI's and for soliciting their support for Sangh Parivar, he says, 'When I wrote 'Hindu Tan Man Hindu Jeevan' I was a student of class X.

Till 1947 I did the RSS work at shakha level ... I also participated in the Quit India movement in 1942 and was jailed (italics added) I was then studying for my Intermediate examination. I was arrested from my native village Bateshwar in Agra district'.

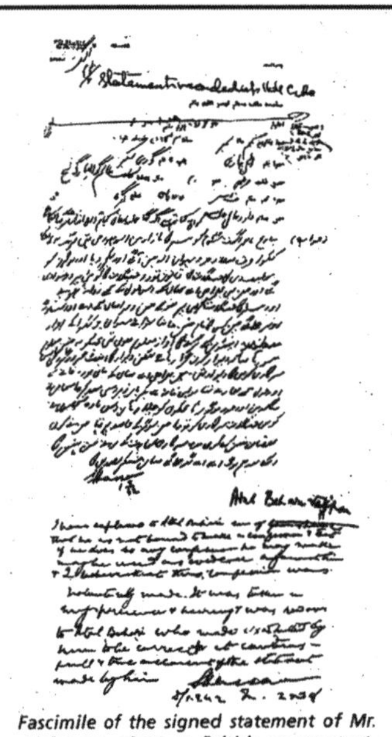

Fascimile of the signed statement of Mr. Vajpayee, given to British government

This claim of his has been investigated in detail and findings published in Frontline Feb. 20, 1998. (Manini Chatterjee and V. K. Ramchandran.)

This investigation nails the lie of his participation in Quit India Movement in 1942. The controversy around his role in the Bateshwar incident comes out very well here.

He had given a confessional statement in the court, which helped in his release from jail for his being just the onlooker and part of the assembly, which went to damage the government property.

As pointed out above he was a dedicated and active member of RSS. He did not participate in the movement according to his own confession, (Frontline, Feb. 20, 1998) and for a brief while was part of the crowd, which went to break the forest law. He could have been prosecuted under section 149 of IPC but for his confession, as the approach of the government was very harsh against the protestors. In his confession he wriggles out of active participation. 'I along with my brother followed the crowd, I did not cause any damage. I did not render any assistance in demolishing the government buildings'.

His statement provided an accurate description of the events on which prosecution could build its case very well. Also it named two leaders of the protesters Kakua alias Liladhar and Mahuan, both of whom were tried in the case. As per Liladhar 'Atal Bihari's confessional statement was not part of the evidence in the court that led to his sentence, but it did help shape the prosecutions case at the investigative stage...prosecution's case largely echoes Atal Bihari's statement.'

Mahatma Gandhi was murdered as he was appeasing the Muslims. This 'appeasement' of Muslims resulted in the partition of the country. On the top of this Gandhi was pressurizing the Govt. to give Rs. 55 crores to Pakistan.

As we will see Gandhi was murdered as he was continuously fighting against the communal forces within both the religions. Godse who had got his initial training in RSS and was editing a paper called Hindu Rashtra murdered Gandhi to further the cause of Hindu Rashtra which is the goal of RSS.

The followers of RSS and Hindu Mahasabha remained aloof from freedom struggle and in all, crucial times collaborated with British. The votaries of Hindu Rashtra, were divided into Hindu Mahasabha, which was more interested in the immediate participation in politics, as the flag bearers of Hindu communal politics, and the RSS which was concentrating on making a network of 'cadres' who could intervene at crucial level by spreading its view in the society. It was bringing in its fold the workers who could later on be useful executioners of Hindutva politics to be ready for the time when the 'real struggle" will begin when the British left and also were spreading the communal venom.

Both these denominations of Hindutva Politics had the common goal of Hindu Rashtra while their goals were common, their social base was common, their key texts were common, but their methods differed. Nathuram Godse, killer of Mahatma 'uniquely' symbolized the fusion of both these trends.

After the murder of Mahatma, the official RSS line had been, 'we have nothing to do with Godse neither is he a member of RSS'. They could get away with this as there was no official record of members of RSS and they could disown Godse at legal level. In 1930 Godse joined RSS and very soon rose to be the Bauddhik Pracharak (intellectual propagator). He was ardent supporter of Akhand Bharat, (undivided India) comprising of today's Pakistan, Bangladesh and Myanmar.

'Having worked for the uplift of the Hindus I felt it necessary to take part in political activities of the country for the protection of just rights of Hindus. I therefore left the Sangh and joined Hindu Mahasabha. (Godse, 'Why I Assassinated Mahatma Gandhi- 1993, and Pg. 102).

As an ardent Hindutvawadi he was extremely critical of Gandhi's ahimsa (non-violence), the movements led by him and thought very lowly of him and scales used to assess him are also very peculiar. His followers cannot see what is clear even to the blind, viz. that Gandhi was a mere pigmy before Shivaji, Rana Pratap and Guru Govind (ibid Pg. 40). According to Godse 'about the winning of swaraj and freedom I maintain the Mahatma's contribution was negligible.' (ibid pg. 87)

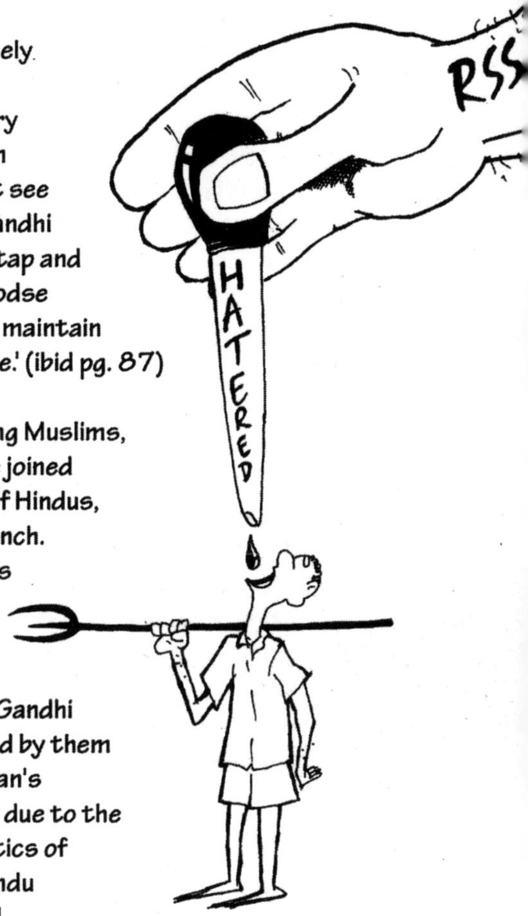

He held Mahatma responsible for appeasing Muslims, and thereby the formation of Pakistan. He joined HM, at that time the only political party of Hindus, and became general secretary of Pune Branch. In due course he founded the newspaper, as founder editor, called Agrani or Hindu Rashtra. Jagan Phadnis in his book 'Mahatmyachi Akher' (Lokvangymay Griha, 1994) argues that Gandhi murder was not on the charges propagated by them (Partition and insistence on paying Pakistan's dues (Rs.55 crore from the treasury) but due to the basic deep differences with the social politics of Gandhi and that of the followers of the Hindu Rashtra. These two reasons are proffered merely as a pretext.

Nathuram Godse was not a member of the RSS.

In an interview given to "The Times of India" (25 Jan. 1998) his brother Gopal Godse, who was also an accomplice in the murder elaborates the apparent reasons and Nathuram's RSS membership.

'The appeasement policy followed by him and imposed on all Congress governments encouraged the Muslim separatist tendencies that eventually created Pakistan and technically and theoretically he (Nathuram) was a member (of RSS), but he stopped working for it later. His statement in the court that he had left the RSS was to protect the RSS workers who would be imprisoned following the murder. On the understanding that they (RSS workers) would benefit from his dissociating himself from the RSS, he gladly did it.

This murder was steeped in both the streams of Hindutva politics, RSS and HM. His editing the paper called, 'Hindu Rashtra' was quite symbolic. This murder had a broad sanction of the followers of HM and RSS, as they celebrated Mahatma's murder by distributing sweets, 'All their (RSS) leaders' speeches were full of communal poison. As a final result of the poisonous atmosphere such a ghastly tragedy (Gandhi's murder) became possible. RSS men expressed their joy and distributed sweets after Gandhi's death. Excerpts from Sardar Patel's letters to M S Golwalkar and S P Mookerjee. (Outlook, April 27, 1998).

They used the word 'wadh' for this murder, which stands for killing a demon who is harming the society. In a way Gandhi's murder was the first major offensive of the Hindutva politics on Indian Nationalism, in a way it was to herald the onset of bigger strides which Hindutva politics was to assume in times to come.

Though officially S.P Mookerjee dissociated from Gandhi's murder by Godse, in private many a members not only uphold the dastardly act, but have even succeeded in undermining the importance of Mahatma and 'sympathise' with Godse.

This complex trick could be achieved only by a multi-headed organization, capable of talking in different tongues at the same time.

HATE IDEOLOGY THAT KILLED GANDHI

I shot Gandhi, I showered him with bullets. I have no regrets. I believe it was right thing to do.

-Nathuram Godse, Hindu Mahasabha, Gandhi's assassin

Our motive was not to achieve control of the government ... we were simply trying to rid the nation of someone who had done and was doing great harm to it. He had consistently insulted the Hindu nation and had weakened it by his doctrine of 'ahimsa'. On his many fasts, he always attached all sorts of pro-Muslim conditions... He never did anything about the Muslim fanatics. We wanted to show Indians that there were Indians who would not suffer humiliation- that there were still men left among the Hindus.

-Gopal Godse, brother of the assassin of Gandhi, Nathuram Godse and a conspirator in the murder, in an interview in Pune on May 13, 1969.

The news of Gandhiji's death caused me no sorrow... Even a simple patriot had begun to oppose his stand vis-a-vis Pakistan and the payment of Rs. 55 crores to it despite its attack on Jammu and Kashmir. His murder was a result of that disenchantment against Gandhiji.

-Vikram Savarkar, Grandson of Veer Savarkar, Hindu Mahasabha

Godse was motivated by (the philosophy) Akhand Bharat. His intention was good but he used the wrong method.

- Rajendra Singh alias Raju Bhayya, RSS Chief on Nathuram Godse, the murder of Mahatma Gandhi, Outlook; April 27,1998

Communalism Combat, February, 1998

RSS has been against the imperialists/colonialists

As we have seen RSS never took part in freedom struggle and was never target of British repression. RSS was banned following Gandhi's murder by Godse. Mr. Golwalkar was put behind bars. Golwalkar wrote a letter from Jail: : "The communists are a great menace to the country. Government's power and RSS network can be combined to weed out this menace." Decades ago M.S. Golwalkar, the then RSS Sarsanghchalak, supremo, had supported the America's aggression on Vietnam. That was the time when most of the World was condemning the US offensive,

its use of inhuman weapons on the unarmed citizens of Vietnam. The pretext for US was that the emerging Vietnamese nationalism is a threat to freedom and democracy, as the flag, which Ho Chi Minh held high was a communist one. While most of the world had problems with the US agenda, RSS chief complimented US as the one, leading the forces of Dharma (Correct moral-ethical values)? It is another matter that RSS certified forces of Dharma had to bite the dust and retreat in a most disgraceful manner. Neither was US trying to protect freedom and democracy nor did RSS supremo mean to defend morals and ethics.

In March 2003, the reigning RSS chief defended the US aggression on Iraq, apparently to liberate the Iraqi people and to install the democracy, which is supposedly the divine mission of Uncle Sam. Mr. Sudarshan upheld George Bush on two grounds. (Times of India, 29th March, 2003) The first one being that it is a clash of civilizations and the backward, retrograde, Jehadi Islamic culture is a threat to the World as a whole and to the advanced, 'humane' Western civilization in particular.

The second one being that Mr. Bush is only defending his own country, as Iraq is a threat to US security. Iraq as per this argument is having weapons of mass destruction and being Muslim; it will support all the terrorists who anyway are Muslims so the US action is justified as per our home bred inheritor of Nazi ideology, the chief of RSS.

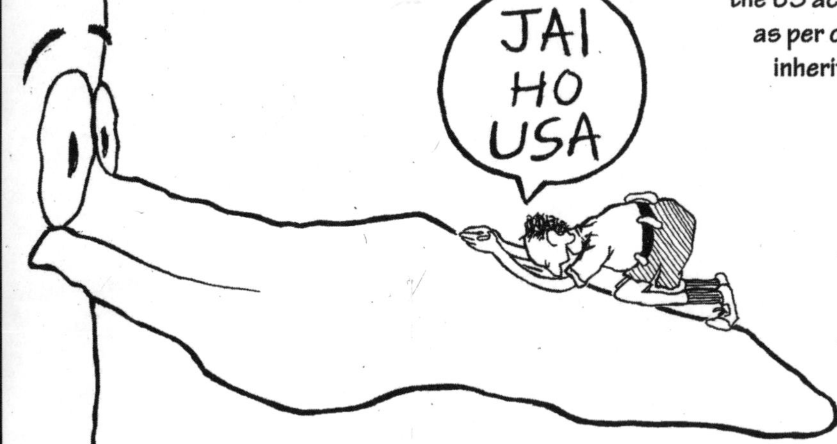

RSS, the proponent of Hindutva, Hindu Rashtra has a very complimentary ideology to the one of colonial powers and imperialists. After Gandhi's murder Mr. Golwalkar, RSS chief requested to be released from jail and promised that RSS will collaborate with the Govt.to eliminate the Communist 'menace'.

Incidentally that was the era when American Imperialism was unleashing McCarthyism and hunting communists. US agenda and RSS agenda matched exactly.

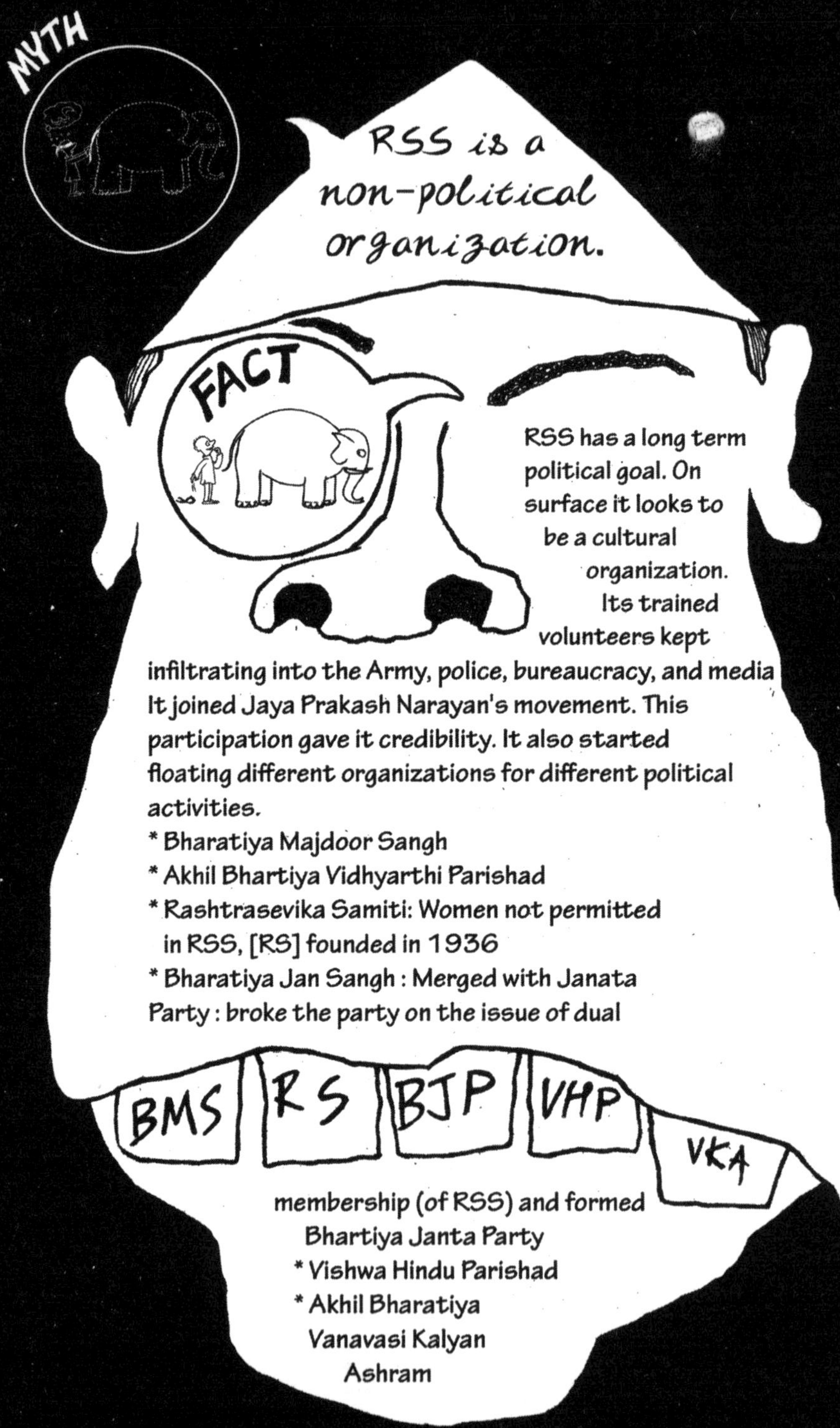
MYTH
RSS is a non-political organization.
FACT
RSS has a long term political goal. On surface it looks to be a cultural organization. Its trained volunteers kept infiltrating into the Army, police, bureaucracy, and media It joined Jaya Prakash Narayan's movement. This participation gave it credibility. It also started floating different organizations for different political activities.
* Bharatiya Majdoor Sangh
* Akhil Bhartiya Vidhyarthi Parishad
* Rashtrasevika Samiti: Women not permitted in RSS, [RS] founded in 1936
* Bharatiya Jan Sangh : Merged with Janata Party : broke the party on the issue of dual
BMS
RS
BJP
VHP
VKA
membership (of RSS) and formed Bhartiya Janta Party
* Vishwa Hindu Parishad
* Akhil Bharatiya Vanavasi Kalyan Ashram

In most of the organizations the 'core' controlling body comes from RSS cadres, others are drawn in on specific issues. RSS control is absolute in these organizations. Now there are over 25000 branches and 3 million members.

- Major landmark in Sangh Parivar (SP) politics:
1. Ban cow slaughter campaign:From the 1960's intermittently even now
2. Regular intimidation of Muslim community through campaigns like 'Indianise Muslims'.
3. Following Shah Bano blunder by govt. Intensification of 'emotive campaigns' by VHP. Ramjanmabhoomi controversy nurtured and 'faith' of 'Hindu' cultivated around Ram Temple in Ayodhya.

Following implementation of Mandal Commission recommendations by V.P. Singh, BJP took up Babri Masjid issue. Advani undertook a 'Rath Yatra' trying to make political capital out of a religious issue for which the ground work done by other wings of Sangh Parivar, leading to the Kar Seva on Dec. 6.

MYTH

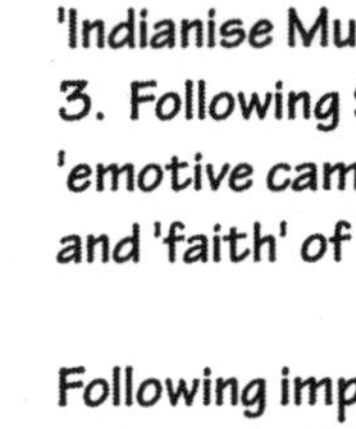

RSS is a democratic organization and Sangh Parivar's aim is Secular Democratic India.

FACT

Sangh Parivar's head RSS is a dictatorial organization, and its politics is directed towards formation of Hindu Rashtra, a goal which is against the existence of democracy and secularism.

Hindu Rashtra vs. Secular Democratic India

Hindu Rashtra	Secular Democratic India
This concept began as the goal of RSS and Hindu Mahasabha, which were not part of the freedom struggle.	This concept evolved as a part of the freedom struggle led by the Indian National Congress. Revolutionaries like Bhagat Singh, Subhash Chandra Bose and of the streams led by Babasaheb Ambedkar stood for this.
Supporters of this concept in the earlier period were Brahmins, Banias, Zamindars and now this gets support from uppercaste and upper-middle class Hindu elite	The supporters: Vast mass of poor peasants, workers , dalits, and sections of Industrialists.
Concept crystallized by ideologues of HIndutva: Savarkar, Golwalkar etc.	Concept enshrined in Indian Constitution which was formed by constituent assembly: fairly representative of Indian people.
This nationalism is based on race, religion and hatred of 'others' on the grounds of race or religion.	Based on recognition of pluralism and geopolitical diversities.
Inherent special status to elite	Based on formal equality of all.
Strengthens 'status quo' based on caste, gender and class	Provision of liberal space to struggle for the rights of the oppressed.
This Society to be guided by Hindu clergy (Mahants, Acharyas) Impose monolithic values and culture on society.	Social life to evolve through mutual interaction of people and communities. Space for plurality. Respect for diversity.
Franchise to be controlled as per the dictates of the elite, the 'self appointed' leaders of 'Hindu society' i.e. by the leaders of the Sangh Parivar	Universal franchise. Everybody has the voting power. All equal in the eyes of law, irrespective of caste, class and gender.
Brahminical norms , elite Sanskritised values to be the 'official', 'mainstream' laws.	Indian Constitution to guide social and political life.
Everybody has to accept 'Hindu' (Brahminical culture)	Communities free to pursue their own culture
Concept close to Mussolini's Italy, Hitler's Germany, Khomeini's Iran and Taliban's Afghanistan	Aspires to be a Democracy: Values of Liberty, Equality and Fraternity for all. Nurtures liberal space.
Hindu elite and co-opted 'other' elite will dominate and dictate terms	Possibility of everybody constituting the political process

THE CONSTITUTION OF INDIA

WE, THE PEOPLE OF INDIA, having solemnly resolved to constitute India into a SOVEREIGN SOCIALIST SECULAR DEMOCRATIC REPUBLIC and to secure to all its citizens:

JUSTICE, social, economic and political;

LIBERTY of thought, expression, belief, faith and worship.

EQUALITY of status and of opportunity;

And to promote among them all

FRATERNITY assuring the dignity of the individual and the unity and integrity of the nation;

IN OUR CONSTITUENT ASSEMBLY this twenty-sixth day of November, 1949, do HEREBY ADOPT, ENACT AND GIVE TO OURSELVES THIS CONSTITUTION.

Doctoring Mass Consciousness

RSS has been active in molecular permeation of concepts and ideas. Projection, propagation and percolation of mythical history to generate a communalized.

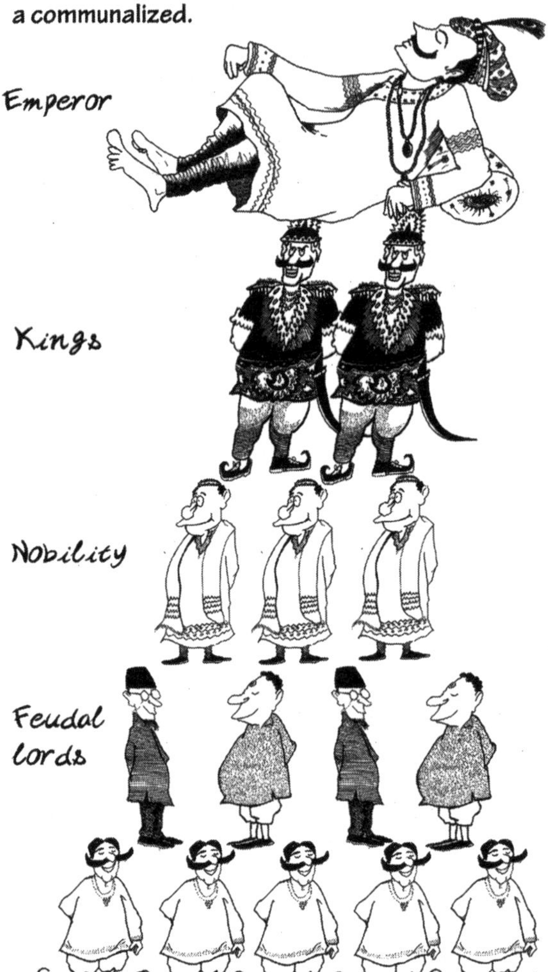

...consciousness has been its major work. It has built upon and strengthened the communal view of history prevalent in the schools, as per which periodization is done on religious basis: Hindu, Muslim and British (not Christian period!).

In Muslim period the ruling structure (Zamindars, Rajas, Courtiers) was constituted both by Hindus and Muslims. Hindus were very much a part of ruling elite during the presently understood Muslim period as well, while the low caste Hindus shared their plight with poor Muslims as the land-less, poor peasants etc.

Different ways of looking at History			
Slave	Ancient		Hindu Period
Feudal	Medieval	Kingdoms	Muslim Period
Bourgeoisie	Modern	Nation States	British Period

Aryans are the original inhabitants of India

The most initial comment on the issue came from Lokmanya Bal Gangadhar Tilak. Tilak believed in Arctic Home of Vedas, that Aryans came from Arctic region. A bit later Golwalkar, in his book, `We or Our Nationhood defined' presented the Aryan race theory in a very different way, to state that Hindus and Hindus alone were the original inhabitants of India. This `core' myth has been constructed by Hindu communalists over a period of last many decades. For Golwalkar, Aryans and Hindus is synonymous, and he goes on to assert that Aryans did not migrate to India from anywhere but originated here.

He had to `deal' with Tilak's theory of `Arctic home of Vedas', and he does it by a perverted and hilarious use of historical fantasies. As per him the "Arctic zone was originally that part of the world which is today called Bihar and Orissa, that then it moved north east and then by a sometimes northward movement, it came to its present position .... We do not hesitate in affirming that had this fact been discovered during the life time of Lokmanya Tilak, he would unhesitatingly have propounded the proposition that `the Arctic home of the Vedas' was verily in Hindustan itself and that it was not the Hindus who migrated to that land but the Arctic zone which emigrated and left the Hindus in Hindustan " (Golwalkar 1939, "We or Our Nationhood Defined" Page 8).

This acrobatics of Hindutva ideologue shows their desperation to somehow prove that Aryans were Hindus as understood today and that they `originated in Hindustan only'. "Even by the logic of his own argument, if the Arctic zone moved away from Bihar-Orissa, how could it leave the people behind who were inhabiting the land mass? When a land mass moves it moves along with everything on it. People cannot be left hanging in a vacuum only to drop down when and where Golwalkar wishes !" (Yechuri, "What is this Hindu Rashtra", Frontline, March 12,1993).

Keeping in mind all the latest archeological findings, and linguistic interpretations, one can say that culture of India goes way back to 6000 B.C. The first most discernible manifestation of which is the Indus valley civilization, which is the most distinct and decipherable civilisation of this region. It declined in the second millennium BC and completely disintegrated by 1500 B.C. when Aryans entered northwest of India.

“The Aryans or Indo-Aryans descendants of the Indo-Europeans had remained for some time in Bactria and the northern Indian plateau, but by about 1500 B.C. they migrated into northern India through passes of Hindu Kush mountains. At first they wandered across the plains of Punjab, searching for pastures, as they were mainly a cattle breeding people. Finally they settled in small village communities in forests and gradually took to agriculture", (Romila Thapar, History of India Vol. I, Pg 38-39. 1966), and went on to produce Rig Veda followed by other Vedic texts.

Contrary to the claims of Hindu communalists Vedic society is no longer regarded the foundation of Indian civilization as a very different Indus civilization already precedes it, and in fact the Indus civilization was more advanced then the following Vedic civilization.

DO YOU WANT TO KNOW?

1. Who were the chief commanders in Shivaji's army?
2. Who was Shivaji's most trusted foreign secretary?
3. What was the name of Shivaji's most trusted servant who was always close to him and helped to escape from Agra?
4. What did Shivaji build right in the front of his palace in Jagadishver temple where he went for daily worship?

Yet why is it when we think of Shivaji today, the betrayal of Afzal Khan and Shivaji's revenge on him (rearing his back open with poisonous nails) is the first thing we think of?

Answers:

1. Daulat khan and Siddi Misri, both muslims 2. Mulla Haider, also a muslim
3. Madani Mehtar, also muslim 4. A special mosque for his muslim subjects to worship.

From Communal Combat

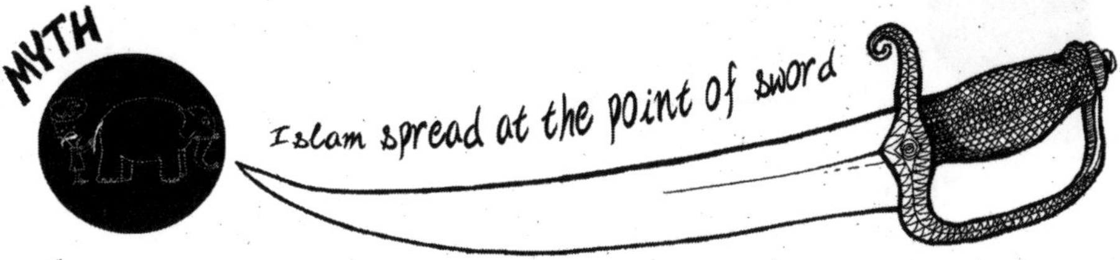

Conversions were not the aim of Kings (except Ashoka). Formation of Muslim community took place in various stages. To begin with it started emerging along Malabar coast when the Arab traders used to come for trade during Seventh Century A.D. They had a religious influence and many people through their interaction took to Islam.

Arab army conquered Sind early in 8th Century, but it had a marginal impact on the society. During 11th and 12th centuries Turkish invasion brought in a larger influence of Islam. Initially this resulted in emergence of Muslim military aristocracy. But this spread was restricted in numbers. Another small trickle came from Hindu upper-classes, some of whom became Muslims either out of conviction, or (mainly) out of hope of reward from the Muslim ruler.

But the main conversions came from the poor low caste untouchables, who despite being the formal part of Hindu fold were under the severe oppression and repression of upper caste Brahmins and Brahminism.

To quote Vivekanand "Why amongst the poor of India so many are Mohammadens? It is nonsense to say that they were converted by the sword. It was to gain liberty from Zamindars and Priests....." (Collected Works-Vol. 8-Page 330). Later the converts swelled in number due to the impact of Sufi saints, who used local customs and rituals to propound humanistic aspects of Islam.

Untouchability is a creation of Islam.

This most blatant myth is propagated by some ideologues of Sangh Parivar(SP), in pursuance of their political project of denigrating Islam and Muslims and to try to co-opt the dalits, and to win over larger sections of `low castes' for electoral purpose. The logic of SP ideologues borders on outright mauling of history in addition to showing their `capacity' to distort the history to no end, to suit (SP) political agenda.'
Singhal (Sunday Observer, 30-7-95) in his interview shows his `understanding' of history as follows, "all communities were equal and enjoyed the same rights (emphasis added) till the advent of Islamic and Christian rule. Humiliation began to be heaped only after the Islamic invasion of our country.

It was because of the repression of different communities that fought the Islamic invaders and defied conversion to Islam that they had to suffer humiliation and torturers. These communities were uprooted from their home and hearth for defying the invaders, and not giving up their religion, they became poor (and) came to be treated as untouchables".

This longish quote demonstrates the depths to which the ideologues of Sangh Parivar can fall to 'doctor' the mass-consciousness in a communal direction. In fact, the truth is something, which exposes the brutality of Brahminical ideology, which is at the core of Hindutva onslaught. First of all, untouchability became the accompaniment of `caste' system, somewhere around first century A.D. Thus, from that time itself untouchability is the social practice prevalent here.

Manusmriti, written in 2nd and 3rd century A.D. codifies the existing practices, which show in utmost clarity the type of despicable social practices, which the upper castes were imposing upon the weaker, lower castes. Now the major incursion, invasions of Muslims begins in the subcontinent from 11 century A.D. and Christian-British colonized South Asia, in 16 - 17 century A.D. The stretch of logic, or the lack of it, by which RSS ideologues can make this assertion, can be understood, only if one suspends the use of one's intelligence during the time, while grappling to understand the `wisdom' of these RSS spokes persons. A late hymn of Rigveda provides mythical origin of the castes: "when the gods made a sacrifice with the man as their victim, when they divided the man, into how many parts did they divide him? What was his mouth, what were his arms, what were his thighs and his feet called. The Brahmin was his mouth, of his arms were made the warrior Kshatriya. His thighs became the Vaishyas, of his feet the Shudra were born." (Thapar, 66, History of India vol. I. Page 39 - 40).

Over a period of time the caste was secured by its being made hereditary and became the basis of eating together and defining marriage limits, etc. By and by the caste based hierarchy rigidified and Shudra castes, became the victim of `pollution-purity' paradigm, dictated by the Brahmins, and was treated as untouchables. These found their reflection in the rigid theories of Manu, whose Manav Dharamashastra (Human Law Code) codified the practices into laws. M.S.Golwalkar upholds Manu, as the first greatest law-maker of mankind, not only for his time, but for all the times to come. The later social struggles to escape the tyrannies of caste system are presented by Ambedkar as revolution and counter-revolution.

He divides the `Pre-Muslim' period into stages of
(a) Brahminism (the Vedic period)
(b) Buddhism connected with rise of first Magadh-Maurya states and representing the revolutionary denial of caste in equalities and
(c) `Hinduism', or the counter revolution, which consolidates Brahmin dominance and the caste heirarchy!
(Gail Omvedt, Dalit Visions pg: 50).

Much before the invasion of Muslim kings Shudras were, treated as untouchables and were the most oppressed and exploited sections of society. The intensity of caste system and untouchability became very intense from post-Vedic to Gupta period. With the foundation of Muslim dynasties new social movements like Bhakti, directly and Sufi, indirectly, partly reduced the intensity of the caste oppression and untouchability.

Later with Christian missionary activities also, the upper caste Hindu outfits felt the threat of `loosing' their grip on the `low castes', and as a response diluted their caste rigidities to the extent of superficially opposing the caste system. Their opposition to caste system comes as a preaching. The best contrast in approach to abolition of caste system and untouchability can be seen in the approaches of Ambedkar and Golwalkar on the issue. The former, holding Manusmriti as the upholder of caste system initiates social movement to burn it, while the latter, around that time writes eulogies for Manu and the system of law provided by him.

Mill has correctly periodized the Indian History into Hindu, Muslim, and British period.

J.S. Mill wrote the book for training British administrators for their posting in India.
He divided the Indian history as
Ancient-----Hindu Period
Medieval----Mughal Period
Modern---- British Period (and not Christian period)

Here history is regarded only as the history of dynasties, and it is supposed that the big chunk of people have no role whatsoever in history making. Even the periodization is totally faulty as in the so called "Hindu period": Mauryas, Indo-Greeks, Shakas, and Kushans, also ruled in different parts of the country. Buddhists also ruled in some parts i.e. there were different rulers in different parts of the country.

Even in the so called Muslim period, the Muslim rule was there only in Northern part of the country, while the boundaries of this kept changing there was no total rule of Muslim kings all over the country. And as we have seen above even in Muslim kings administration there were number of Hindu kings and Zamindars (Feudal Lords) as a part of the administration.

DO YOU WANT TO KNOW?

1. Who conferred a Jagir and cash gift on the temple Someshwar Nath Mahadev in Allahabad municipality?
2. Who conferred grants to the Mahakeshwar temple in Ujjain, the Balaji temple in Chitrakoot, the Umananda temple in Gauhati and the Jain temple of Shatrunjaya and the other gurudwras scattered in the northern India.
3. What happened when Tanashah, the ruler of Golconda, after collecting the revenues of the state did not pay his dues to Delhi that accumulated into crores and buried this treasure and erected the Jama Masjid over it?

Yet, the first image that gets conjured up when we think of Aurangzeb is of a single minded temple breaker and a destroyer of idols.

If this image that we have of Aurangzeb, is not the truth, why not look at history and find out for ourselves what our kings and queens, saints and poets actually did or said about each other?

Answers

1. *Aurangzeb, with the words that "the jagir was being transferred for the pooja and bhog of the deity."*
2. *Aurangzeb, through farmans issued from 1659 AD to 1091 AD.*
3. *Aurangzeb, ordered the demolition of the mosque, seized the treasure and utilized it for the benefit of the people.*

DO YOU WANT TO KNOW?

1. Name the only Indian ruler who died fighting the British.
2. Name the only Indian ruler who had created the institution of Devauthtadamayaka (an officer for uprooting of Gods/temples)
3. In which classical Indian text is the function of Devauthtadamayaka described?

Answers

1. *Tipu Sultan*
2. *King Harshadev of Kashmir*
3. *Kalhana's Rajatarangini*

Courtesy: Communalism Combat

Muslim Kings destroyed Hindu Temples

Plunder of Temples was done by Kings (irrespective of their religion). Temples were repositories of wealth. Ideological veneer was drawn from religion for plundering acts. Temples were plundered by Marathas in Tipu's sultanate. The Shrirangapatanam temple was destroyed by Maratha armies and was repaired by Tipu Sultan.

Attacking the temple was a way of humiliating the other kings. The famous temple of Somnath was looted by Muhammed Gazani. His main aim in this was to loot the tons of gold kept in the temple. On his way to Somnath he first had to fight with Muhammed Fath Dawood and in the process the mosque of Multan was damaged. Further on he allied with Anadpal the ruler of Thaneshwar, before attacking the temple. Many of his army generals (Tilak, Sondhi, Rai Hind and Harzan were Hindus and a substantial part of his army was constituted by Hindu soldiers). Later his son sent his army to destroy a mosque in central Asia.

Temples were also looted by King Harsha (Kashmir), in the 11th century Kashmir. The mention of this is found in Kalhan's book "Rajtarangini", which says that he appointed a special officer to uproot the gold idols from the temples. This officer was designated as Devotpatan Nayak' (officer who uproots the Gods). Parmar Kings destroyed Jain temples. Similarly Aurangzeb not only destroyed some temples and mosques, he also gave Jagirs to many a temples.

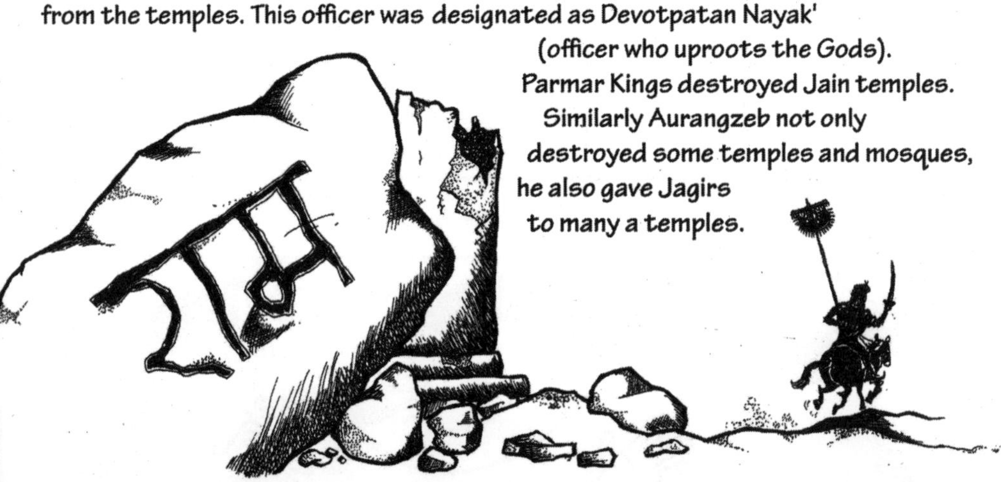

In medieval times Hindus and Muslims kept fighting with each other.

Large number of courtiers, Rajas and Zamindars were Hindus and the existing social structure was not disturbed. Hero myths also generated communalism.

All the Hindu kings who fought for 'their' kingdoms against the Muslim empire, are projected as 'national heroes': Shivaji, Rana Pratap, Guru Govind Singh. Many of them and their descendants 'allied' with Mughal rulers e.g. Rana Pratap's son Amar Singh developed friendship with Jehangir, in later period Guru Gobind Singh came to an agreement with Mughal rulers.

ALLIANCE		
	Against	
Akbar+Man Singh	x	Rana Partap + Hakim Sur
Aurangzeb+ Mirza Raja Jaisingh	x	Shivaji+ Pathan Muslims in army, Ibrahim Gardi Chief of Canon Division. Muslim as Chief Secretary (Maulvi Hyder Ali)
Babar + Rana Sanga	x	Babar + Rana Sanga

BABAR'S WILL

Son, this Nation Hindusthan has different religions. Thank Allah for giving us this Kingdom. We should remove all the differences from our heart and do justice to each community according to its customs. Avoid cow-slaughter to win over the hearts of the people of this land and to incorporate the people in the matters of administration. Don't damage the places of worship and temples, which fall in the boundaries of our rule.

Evolve a method of ruling whereby all the people of the kingdom are happy with the King and the King is happy with the people. Islam can progress by noble deeds and not by terror. Ignore the differences of Shia and Sunni as this is the weakness of Islam. Keep the people following different customs integrated into a single whole so that no part of the body of this Kingdom becomes diseased.

(Translated from the original in the National Museum)

The 'credit' of breaking temples is shared by
us along with them
We have also broken temples of Jains, Buddhists
And erected temples of Ram, Hanuman.
For establishing the religion state
We unleashed crusades also
The punya of killing those belonging to other
religions is shared by us also
it was our Pushyamitra Shung, who changed the
colour of earth from black to saffron, with the
blood of thousands of innocent monks.

-Alok Bhattacharya

WHY VISHWANATH TEMPLE WAS DEMOLISHED?

There are instances which prove beyond doubt that Aurangzeb did order demolition of Vishwanath temple at Varanasi and the Jama Masjid at Golkunda and the reasons that were given out for the demolition of the temple and the mosque may give benefit of circumstances to Aurangzeb.

The story regarding Vishwanath temple is that while Aurangzeb was passing near Varanasi on his way to Bengal, the Hindu Rajas in his retinue requested that if the halt was made for a day their Ranis may go to Varanasi, have a dip in the Ganges and pay their homage to Lord Vishwanath. Aurangzeb readily agreed. Army pickets were posted on the five mile route to Varanasi. The Ranis made the journey on the palkis. They look their dip in the Ganges and went to the Vishwanath temple to pay their homage. After offering puja all the Ranis returned except one, the Maharani of Kutch. A thorough search was made of the temple precincts but the Rani was to be found nowhere. When Aurangazeb came to Know of it he was very much enraged. He sent his senior officers to search for Rani.

Ultimately they found that the statue of Ganesh which was fixed in the wall was moveable one. When the statue was moved, they saw a flight of stairs that led to the basement. To their horror, they found the missing Rani dishonoured and crying. The basement was just beneath Lord Vishwanath's seat. The Rajas demanded exemplary action. Aurangazeb ordered that as the sacred precincts have been despoiled, Lord Vishwanath may be moved to some other place. The temple be razed to the ground and the Mahant arrested and punished.

Dr. Pattabhi Sitaramayya, in his famous book, "The Feathers and the Stones" has narrated this fact based on documentary evidence. Dr. P. L. Gupta, Former Curator of Patna Museum, has also corroborated this incident.

The farmans of Aurangzeb on Hindu Temples

By Bishamber Nath Pande

Excerpts from the Booklet Published by Centre for Study of Society and Secularism, Mumbai. Mr. Bishamber Nath Pande is a Member of Rajya Sabha and former Governer of Orissa. He is a constant campaigner against communalism and has been writing on historical aspects of communalism.

"Though these are only a few instances of Aurangzeb's generous attitude towards Hindus and their temple, they are enough to show that what the historians have written about him are biased and is only one side of the picture" (p 2)

"Aurangzeb seemed to be very careful to respect the religious sentiments of his subjects.That Aurangzeb had the attitude of tolerance towards Hindus and their religion, is further supported by the priests of the Mahakaleshwar temple at Ujjain" (p 8)

"These two examples are sufficient to show that Aurangzeb did not make any distinction between a temple and a mosque, in the matter of judicial finding" (p13).

Hindutva and Exploited, Oppressed Sections of Society

A. Workers:

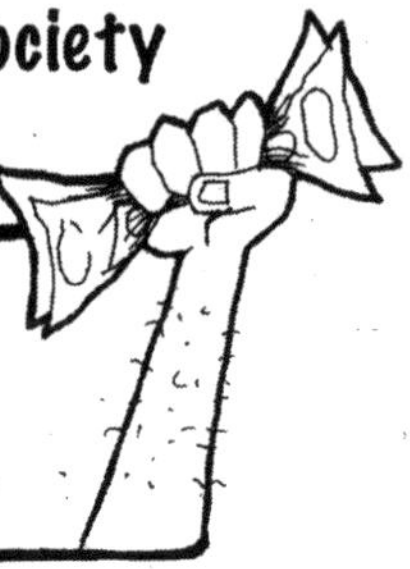

RSS labour wing Bharatiya Mazdur Sangh (BMS) was formed to protect the interests of workers.

During independence struggle, workers were organized by communists. Communist party was the major opposition party; their ideology is based on the understanding of irreconcilability of class interests', 'class war' and 'haves' and 'have-nots' ideas. Sangh Parivar founded Bharatiya Mazdoor Sangh (BMS) to counter the influence of communists amongst workers.

BMS rejects class struggle theory and is critical of capitalist greed for profit but not of the system which gives rise to the capitalists and their absolute control over means of production. It puts forward the 'Hindu' alternative, the ideal of converting enterprises into occupational families (i.e. accepting the inherent patriarchal power relations in an enterprise). Workers are to participate in management under the patriarchal supervision of industrialists. As per BMS, workers should cultivate harmonious relations with the owners of enterprises. BMS rejects international solidarity of labour.

In practice BMS operates as a 'milder' form of TU especially amongst 'white collar' workers. It never undertook any militant struggles. Also it mobilized workers for 'Kar Seva' to demolish the Babri Masjid. It is conspicuous by its absence amongst agricultural labour, poor peasants and adivasi struggles. Currently its major demand is that for swadeshi, which does favour the small and local industrialists but is totally quiet about the condition of workers in these 'swadeshi' enterprises. These 'swadeshi' enterprises practice extremely repressive methods in their dealing with the workers, their working conditions and the wages are abysmally bad.

(B) Women

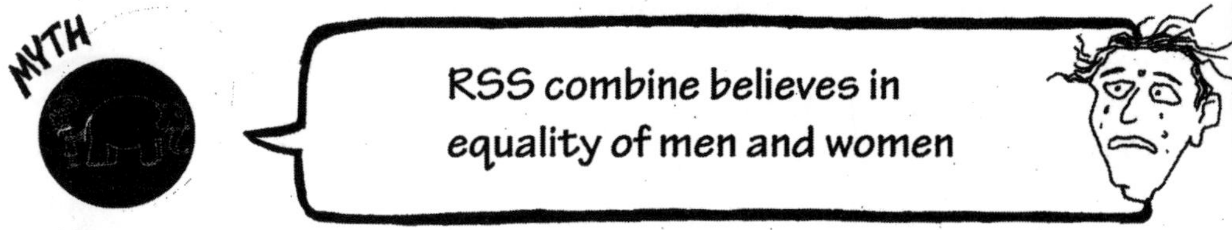

Women relatives of RSS members wanted to join RSS, an exclusively male organization, they were advised to form a separate Rashtrasevika Samiti (Note: RSS is a National Volunteers Organisation , whereas RS means committee of Servants of the Nation. This was formed in 1936.

It draws subtly from Manusmriti, where womb is equated to a field, in which men sow seed, making the produce of the field theirs. Women are understood as dependents and under protection of father, husband and son, in different stages of their life. Women are denied access to Upanayan (beginning of sacred learning of males), for women marriage is prescribed as a substitute for learning and serving husband, running the household is equated to studentship.

As per Golwalkar disparity is an indivisible part of nature and we have to live with it, harmony and not equality should be the organizing principle of society according to him. Women should primarily be 'ideal' mothers and bring up children within RSS framework of Samskaras (rituals). A.B. Vajpayee in an interview to Hindi weekly Dharmyug (1990) said that "Women who want to become like men are worth ridiculing". SP regards women to be primarily mothers in their social role. The subordinate position of women gets reflected in various ways.

Mridula Sinha, ex-President of BJP Mahila Morcha in an interview in Savvy, April 1994, states that

One of the past Vice-Presidents of BJP and a prominent functionary of BJP Mahila Morcha, Vijaya Raje Scindia, led a band of supporters in a protest march against 'anti-Sati' legislation, asserting that, 'It is the fundamental right of Hindu women to commit Sati, as it is in preservation of our past glory and culture. Nearly 20,000 'Kar Sevikas' helped the 'Kar Sevaks' assembled to demolish the masjid, by cooking and cleaning for them.

Some of the women belonging to different 'Women Wings' of SP-Shiv Sena exhorted their male 'brethren' to participate in communal violence in Bombay.

The Rashtrasevika Samiti has ambivalent stand on dowry and bride burning. Samiti members help each other to raise the dowry. They disapprove of divorce and there is no provision of legal counseling to women fighting against their families for their rights. In response to coming into newer space of social life, SP straightjackets their role as ideal mothers and wives, subordinate to the males. They do not have any concept of women's rights.

MYTH

Women had a very honorable place in the past, and SP wants to restore this place to the Hindu Women.

FACT

While propagating these Hindutva votaries purposefully forget the place, which Hindu women had in the past. This is very well depicted by Manusmriti, which spells out that woman is a property of man and she has to 'loyally' serve him irrespective of his whims and fancies.

Hindutva votaries : (forgetting Manusmriti) concoct that women had a more honorable place in Hindu society, its only to protect them from being the 'prey' of aliens that restrictions on their social life were imposed. SP wants to relegate women's place as subordinate to that of men in the society.

C. Dalits

Savarkar and Ambedkar had similar approach to the caste system

RSS is making a great attempt to appropriate and iconize Ambedkar and these assertions are a part of that. Savarkar opposed the caste system but did not support or participate in any of the campaigns against untouchability launched by Ambedkar.

BJP/RSS want to equate Savarkar and Ambedkar, as their teachings being similar, both wanted to reform Hindu society. Savarkar did not want reforms without supporting the natural rights of human beings, nor did he fight against social oppression.
Ambedkar stood for liberty, equality, fraternity and democracy and organized untouchables to fight for their social and economic rights.
Similarly Ambedkar's attempts to get entry into temples also went unsupported by the Hindutva votaries who today are claiming to be opposed to these practices.

The RSS and Ambedkar both wanted to reform Hindu society.

Ambedkar made all the efforts to struggle against the humiliating treatment given to Sudras in Hindu society. His campaigns to get access to public drinking water (Chavadar Talav, Mahad), Manusmriti Dahan and Kalaram Temple, none of these were supported by the RSS and Hindu Mahasabha.

He undertook to burn Manusmriti, while Golwalkar chose to write eulogies for the same book. As per Golwalkar, Manu is the first and greatest law-giver of the world, whose code has asked all people all over the world to learn wisdom from traditional Brahmins. Manu had converted the division of labour into caste system.

As per which the only duty of Shudra is to serve Brahmins, who in turn should give him left-over food, discarded clothes and utensils. If Shudras try to study, their tongue should be chopped off and if they happen to hear the noble 'Vedas', molten lead should be poured into their ears. The Purush Sukta states that Brahmins are the head, Kshatriyas are the arms, Vaishyas are the groin and Shudras, the feet.

Movement against untouchability was never on the agenda of RC. In December 1992 Dharam Sansad of VHP passed a resolution stating that- Indian constitution is non-Hindu and should be replaced by a 'Hindu constitution'. For SP Manusmriti has provided justice to all, its laws are more important than Constitution of India. Ambedkar states that, Hindus are neither a nation nor are they a society.

The reality of social life of Hinduism is caste system because of which there is a lack of dialogue and opportunities in cultural life, and there is no feeling of togetherness. Due to social, economic and educational contradictions the society of Hindus cannot become a nation.

After his initial support to the idea of Pakistan on the grounds that Muslims are a separate nation, he realised that formation of Pakistan would increase the possibility of Hindu Raj (SP's Hindu Rashtra). This realization made him change his opinion saying that 'If Hindu Raj does become a fact, it will no doubt be the greatest calamity of this country. No matter what the Hindus say, Hinduism is a menace to liberty. Hindu Raj must be prevented at any cost.

The inadequacy of policies of the previous government has resulted in the failure to bridge the social gap between the low caste/oppressed class and other sectors of society. Mandalisation has unleashed a process of assertion by the lower castes and OBC's, frightened by this the upper castes are equating 'casteism' with the communalism. Communalism is the virus spearheading the interests of the elite of society, the upper castes. The casteism of lower castes has an anti-exploitative, liberatary potential, a potential to usher in secularization, a potential to strengthen democratic norms in society. It gives them an identity, a ground to struggle for their social and economic rights. On the face of it RSS asserts equality, but in a subtle way it sustains the chronic, low intensity warfare against the lower castes. BJP has couched its views and attitudes towards Dalits in a very clever way. It will not criticize dalits but whenever faced with their movements, demands and cultural upsurge, it will start beating the drum of abolishing reservations and upholding merit. There is a whispering campaign against reservations for Dalits. It could not 'oppose' Mandal for electoral reasons, so it decided to distract the social focus to 'Ram Temple'. Despite the assertions of SP, Dalits have realized the designs of SP, and except few upwardly mobile elements from amongst them others do not fall prey to their 'social engineering' tactics.

RSS Sarsanghchalak is correct in saying that Ambedkar supported RSS ideology.

Sudarshan's assertion that Ambedkar drafted a Western constitution under the pressure of Congress, insults Dr. Ambedkar in a deeper way. Ambedkar was not the one to buckle under pressure. He had the values and ideas of his own, and the example of this was when he resigned from the Cabinet because Hindu Code Bill drafted by him did not pass through and also because he was side tracked in other matters of policy and planning.

It's a comment which is derogatory to the thinker and leader who did all possible to ensure that he stands for his values and ideas rather than compromises for the sake of power and self. At the same time Sudarshan seems to be promoting his own postulate that Indian Constitution, is based on Western values and should be replaced by the one based on Hindu holy books. It is in that direction that BJP led NDA coalition appointed the Constitution Review Committee, which of course was a dismal failure, thanks to the opposition of RSS formulation by most of the people of this country.

Ambedkar did not buckle under anybody's pressure while drafting the Constitution as he was committed to the democratic values of Liberty, Equality and Fraternity (community), the ones which have been enshrined in this book. Also it was the constituent assembly, a reasonably accurate representative body of Indian people, which guided the Constitution and not the Western influence. One can go on to say that the Constitution itself was one of the major contributions of Babasaheb.

Sudarshan also asserts that Dr. Ambedkar stuck to Hindu culture while embracing Buddhism. Nothing could be farther from truth. By no stretch of imagination one can call all the tendencies prevailing in India as Hindu. The dominant tradition, which passes off as Hinduism is Brahmanism.

Dr. Ambedkar called Hinduism as Brahminic theology and went on to say that he was born a Hindu that was not in his hands, but surely he will not die a Hindu. Buddhism is not a part of Hindu culture. The central part of dominant Hinduism is caste system, while Buddhism stands for social equality.

As per Ambedkar the clash between Brahminic Hinduism and Buddhism is the major part of Indian history. In his understanding of Indian history he divides it into three parts. Part one: Revolution, i.e. coming in of Buddhism to oppose Brahminic caste and gender hierarchies. Part two: counterrevolution, during which Brahminism attacks Buddhism at ideological level through Shankaracharya. Part three: at the social and political level by the onslaughts of kings like Pushmitra Shunga and Shashank. It is due to this that Buddhism became extinct from India till Dr. Ambedkar brought it back.

He chose this religion, while rejecting Hinduism, mainly because its values of Liberty, Equality and Fraternity (Community). To present him as supporter of RSS and RSS ideology is a clever deceit, a political move, to win over sections of Dalits to RSS-Hindutva politics.

Ambedkar was anti Muslim!

Pursuing this aggressive Hindutva Mr. Katiyar (BJP leader) has been going hammer and tongs spreading Anti-Muslim sentiments. And to buttress his venom he has been using the selective quotations from Ambedkar's writings showing him as anti-Muslim. One can safely say that Ambedkar was giant of an intellectual with prolific contribution on different aspects on Indian politics. His writings and speeches spread over 16 volumes cover practically all the aspects of social and political problems faced by India. He wrote with depth and went to the root of problems.

What are being misused are the selective quotes from his books on Partition. A complete reading of the book reveals that he studied the problem in its multiple dimensions and in his summary he went on to say two major things. "Strange as it may appear Mr. Savarkar and Mr. Jinnah, instead of being opposed to each other on the one nation versus two nations issue, are in complete agreement about it. Both agree and not only agree but insist that there are two nations in India- one the Muslim nation and the other the Hindu nation." He continues, "They differ only as regards the terms and conditions on which the two nations should be. Jinnah says India should be cut up into two, Pakistan and Hindustan, the Muslim nation to occupy Pakistan and the Hindu nation to occupy Hindustan.

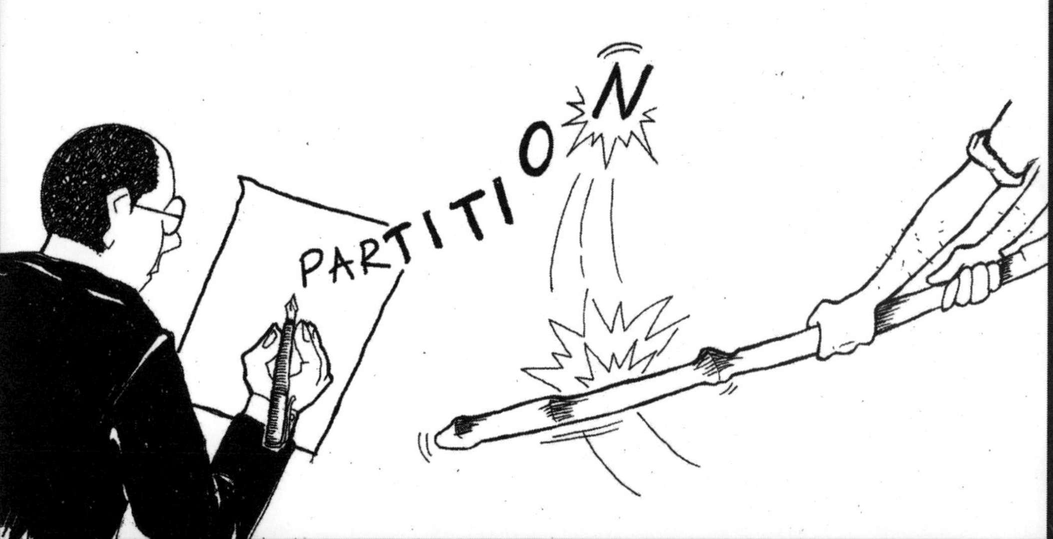

Mr. Savarkar on the other hand insists that, although there are two nations in India, India shall not be divided into two parts, one for the Muslims and the other for Hindus; that the two nations shall dwell in one country and shall live under the mantle of one single Constitution: that the Constitution shall be such that the Hindu nation will be enabled to occupy a predominant position that is due to it and the Muslim nation to be made to live in the position of subordinate co-operation with the Hindu nation." (Thoughts on Pakistan, Third section, chapter VII)

He was for composite Indian Nationalism, "Is it not a fact that under the Montague Chelmsford reforms in most provinces, if not in all, the Muslims, the non-Brahmins and Depressed Classes united together and worked for the reforms as members of one team from 1920 to 1937? Herein lay the most fruitful method of achieving communal harmony among Hindus and Muslims and of destroying the danger of Hindu Raj. Mr. Jinnah could have easily pursued this line. Nor was it difficult for Mr. Jinnah to succeed in it." (Thoughts on Pakistan, P. 359).

Rather than being anti Muslim, he tried to project that both these Hindu and Muslim Nationalism are not the democratic Nationalism. While chairing the drafting committee of Indian Constitution he picked up the principles, which were totally opposed to the ideologies of communal Nationalism. In addition he was concerned about safeguards for minorities and Dalits both.

(D) Adivasis

Adivasis have their own culture. They practice nature worship and are animists.

From 1987, the RSS has activated its offshoot Vanvasi Kalyan Ashram (VKA) into higher gear of activity. Adivasis, the most neglected part of society, are being wooed through newly devised cultural mechanisms.

To begin with Vanvasi Kalyan Ashram used the word Vanvasi, instead of the correct nomenclature, Adivasi. The claim put forward by Hindutva is that these are parts of Hindu society who went to jungles to escape the conversion by Muslim kings. Due to their long stay in jungles they became untouchables and drifted away from the fold of Hindu society. This assertion kills many birds in one stone. On one side it tries to project that despite Aryans coming here from outside, Arctic zone, are not foreigners like the Muslims and Christians. Then aggressiveness of Muslim kings is restated and the inner cruelty of Brahminical Hinduism is hidden as Adivasi 'problem' is projected to be coming from outside. A shifting of the 'blame' of inner ills to outside forces! Another aim achieved through this formulation is to bring Adivasis to Hindu fold and claim that its not a conversion but mere Ghar Vapasi, (returning home), of these wretched of the earth. At the same time for the political project of intimidating the Christian missionaries working in the villages, a ground is prepared to attack them as foreigners.

The forays of Sangh in Adivasi areas intensified from mid eighties when it was realized that by directly attacking Dalits, the way they were attacked in 1980 and 1986 in Gujarat through caste violence, will be counter-productive at electoral level. The strategy evolved was to 'use' them as foot soldiers against Muslim minorities. At the same time electoral arithmetic brought to their attention this substantial chunk of population of Adivasis trying to come up through modern education and thereby disturbing the status quo, prevalent in the far off villages.

Its here that the Christian missionaries were perceived as a big threat to the project of Sangh, which wants to maintain status quo vis-a-vis Adivasis, Dalits and women. Through the network of schools spread in the far off areas these Missionaries were/are instrumental in getting a section of Adivasis empowered and in the process the upper caste affluent base of Sangh was/is getting jittery.

The posting of RSS volunteers into the forest work was very systematic. Apart from attacking the Christian missionaries as foreigners the Ghar Vapasi was brought in at a big scale in all the Adiviasi areas scattered from Gujarat to MP to Orissa. Around this time many a swamis, descended in these areas, Lakkhanand in Phulbani area, Aseemanand in Dangs, Asaram disciples in Jhabua and many other such efforts were unleashed.

In Adivasi areas they resorted to intimidation, you are Hindus, Hindu rituals are like this and so these have to be part of your life. Dilip Singh Judeo, of the 'God is money' fame, of Chattisgarh, had the record number of Adivasis converted into Hinduism by newly devised baptizing techniques.

At the same time Hanuman was popularized as the God in this area and lately Shabri, the destitute woman who had the privilege of offering wild berries to Lord Ram is being projected as the Goddess of Adivasis. The cultural symbolism cannot be missed in the selection of these deities. Hanuman was the unquestioning devotee of Lord Ram, with muscular power as the main virtue. He is capable of flying while carrying a huge mountain. But all the more he is carrying the mountain because he cannot identify the herb needed for treatment of Laxman, Lord's younger brother.

This is what is the signal to Adivasis unquestioning loyalty to Lord Ram, no need to have education. So what are the Christian missionaries doing here? Why should they be trying to educate you? They are foreigners. So Pastor Stains is picked up for the treatment which they want meted out to the white robed priests and nuns.

Shabri, the embodiment of poverty is being glorified on purpose. Your great ancestress had the privilege to offer wild berries to the Lord. She is your role model, poor, powerless and with blind reverence and devotion for the upper caste.

The recently held festival in Subir, Dang district of Gujarat, celebrated Shabri and lakhs of Advasis were brought from neighbouring Adivasi areas for the festival. The local people were scared that Sangh's festival may create the trouble and they may try to forcibly do the conversions to Hinduism. It was declared that Christians and Muslims are foreigners and are a threat to Hindu religion. This Kumbh is meant to protect the Hindus from the foreigners. In the beginning it was announced that conversions are the aim of Kumbh and then silence was kept on this point once various groups questioned their motives. This was boldly stated in the CD produced by Shabri Kumbh organizers. By the time the court ruling came to ban this CD was given, lakhs of its copies were already circulated and had the desired effect of threatening the Christian community.

The Shabri Samiti distributed saffron flags to the villagers and spread the word that those who do not put the flag will be regarded as anti-Hindu, those who do not visit the Kumbh will also be regarded as anti-Hindu. In this intimidating atmosphere the intervention of Human rights groups resulted in the Central government sending its observers. Also the Adivasi leaders realized the game being played by Sangh and mercifully a large section of native Adivasis kept away from the festival. But Sangh has succeeded in spreading the seeds of hate and intimidation far and wide.

The native Adivasi festivals and Gods are being undermined in various ways. Adivasis never used to have the temple or place of prayer within four walls, most of their Gods were in the open. The festivals, dancing and feasting also were held in the open. With the new influence things are changing. The rift between the 'Hindu' and 'Christian' Adivasis is widening which surely will have adverse impact on the life in the area. In pursuance of the same tactics, now Summer Festival and Anjani Mahotsav (festival) are being planned. Anjani, mother of Hanuman was never the object of veneration. Now she will be occupying a place amongst the deities.

From the villages young girls in the age groups of 14-15 are being picked up to be trained as Sadhvis who can give recitation of Ramayana and other Hindu scriptures. The whole emphasis is on the cultural manipulation and the basic issues of Adivasis like land, education and health are being cleverly sidetracked through this culturo-religious manipulation.

One can see the social engineering in practice. The positive experience is that it seems that intervention of Human rights groups can partly change the direction of events in a healthy direction.

Just before the Kumbh, human rights teams had investigated and put out a resort, which was taken note of by the authorities and local leaders. This put the Gujarat Government and Hindutva forces on the defensive. The expected turnout did not materialize and even the Ghar Vapasi was muted. The scare amongst the minorities in such areas has been intensified.

(E) Minorities

1. Muslims

At the time of the partition of the country, the elite of Muslim community left India for Pakistan, and mainly poor Muslims and only few professionals and traders were left behind. There was further worsening of the status of Muslims, Muslim fundamentalists came to the fore, unconcerned about the 'real' material problems of community, which resulted in the community remaining mainly poor, backward and in the grip of orthodox elements.

Successive governments pampered and appeased the community.

Their status in employment and other parameters are a good index of their social status and appeasement.

Muslim Employment in Central Government Services : 2000			
Group	Estimated Strength	Percentage of total strength	Muslim representation in 1992 (in %)
A	77,680	2.05	1.61
B	1,74,675	4.63	3.00
C	23,87,625	63.22	4.41
D	11,36,686	30.09	5.12
Total	37,76,666	100.00	-
Source: Omar Khalidi, Muslims in the Indian Economy, Three Essays Collective, P. 45, New Delhi, 2006			

The Sachar Committee appointed by the Govt. highlighted the economic, social and political plight of Muslim community.

Muslim Employment in Central Government Services

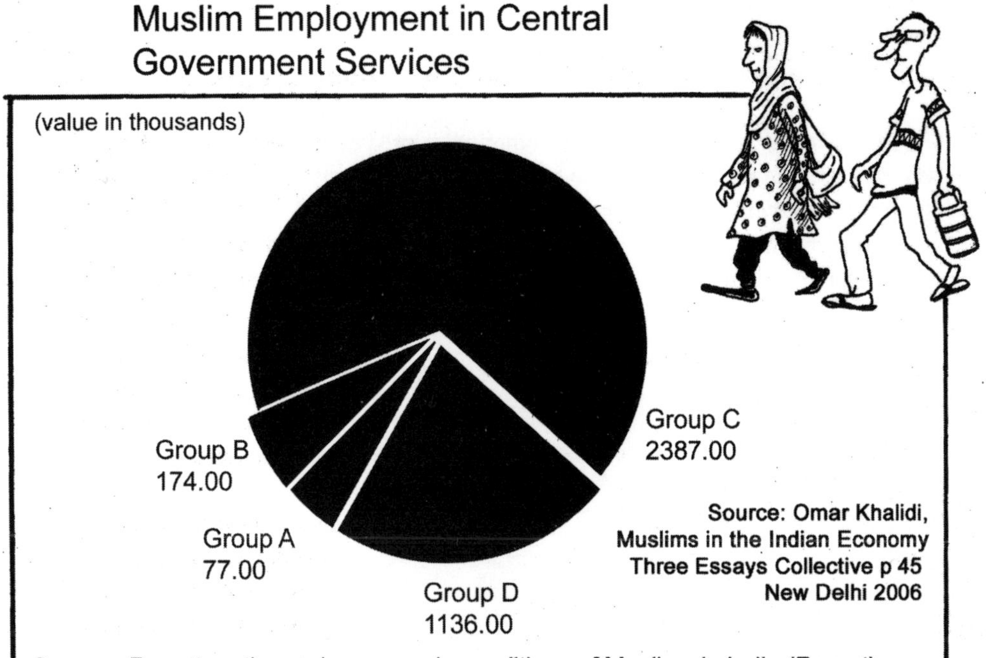

Source : Report on the socio-economic conditions of Muslims in India (Report) by Action Aid (AA), Jahangirabad Media Institute (JMI) & Indian Social Institute (ISI)

Representation of Muslims in the14th Lok Sabha

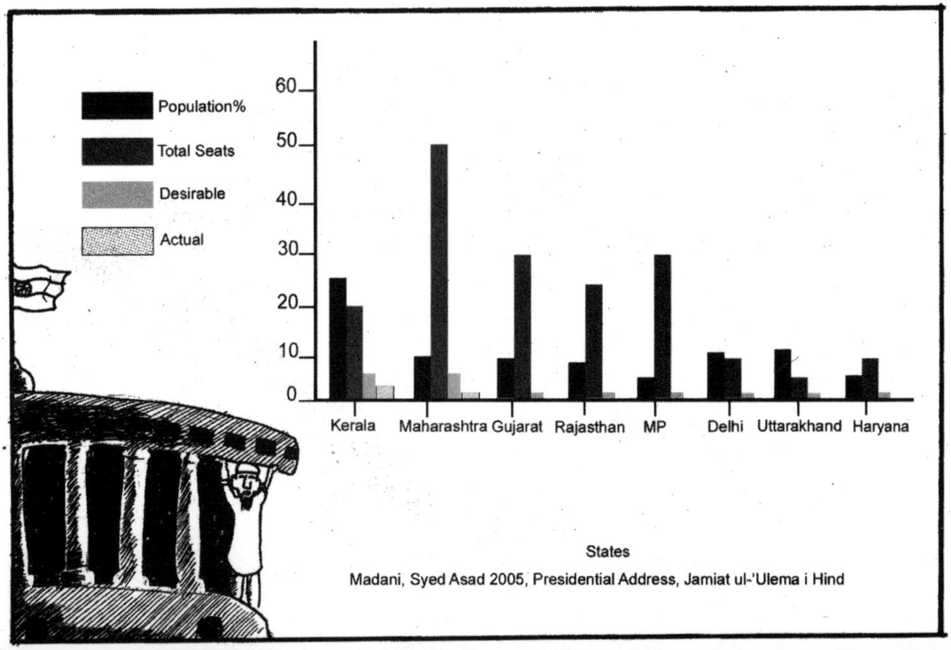

Madani, Syed Asad 2005, Presidential Address, Jamiat ul-'Ulema i Hind

Comments on Rajinder Sachar Committee Data

The only concern shown for Muslim community has been only in the matters of security and appeasement of the Maulanas. Muslims are grossly underrepresented in all sectors of employment and social facilities. Their under-representation in Judiciary, prosecutors, coupled with the rank poverty and marginalization in society has resulted in their 'over representation'

as those accused in cases or jailed on some or the other charges. While Muslim population is 13.4%, amongst jail inmates they are 23.4%,

Justice Varma remarks " Its not the democracy alone that can sustain a society like India. It has to be an inclusive democracy.

All sections of society have to be properly represented and have a voice in all aspects of governance. and policy making. Democracy today is not just the rule of brute majority. It can last and be resilient only if all sections of society are co-opted and taken along." (Indian Express, 28th Oct, 2006).

Chief Information Commissioner Wajahat Habibullah says, 'Higher number of Muslims in jails is also a reflection of the fact that Muslims are poorer generally and are more likely to be picked on by the police because they are easy prey due to fewer entitlements. Prejudice amongst them also exists but gets compounded because of poverty.' Syed Shahabuddhin points out, 'Its like the Afro-Americans in the US. Their proportionate share in jails is much more than their population-share. Less opportunities in the formal channels is one of the reasons for some of them putting in their best to shine in films, music and sports. This also may be the reason for some of them ending up in crime.

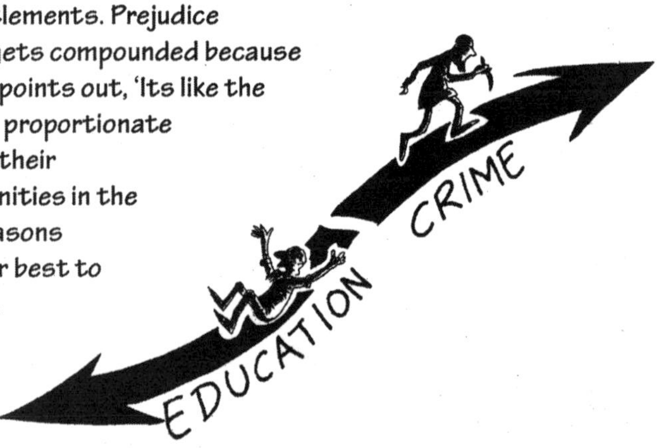

Sachar Committee data shows that Muslims are worse off than Scheduled castes, when it comes to education they significantly lag behind Other Backward Classes (OBCs) virtually in every field, education and employment amongst them poverty levels are comparatively higher and land holdings lower.

Muslims in Private Sector

In the private sector, including the two top business and industrial houses of the Tatas and Birlas, it was found that the Muslim employment came to 8.16%, while for the Scheduled Castes it was 11.5%. In the executive cadre Muslims were only 1.5% while in the clerical class it was 8.28%.

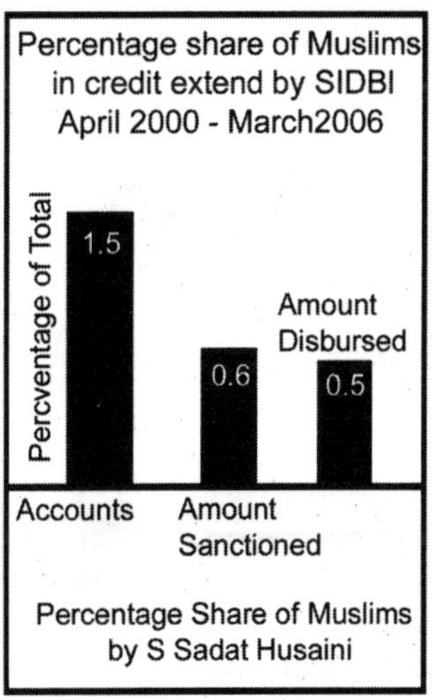

Muslims: Socio Economic Condition

Muslims have also not been able to take advantage of various government schemes for such groups as small farmers, marginal farmers, agricultural labourers, landless labourers, etc.. This owes to discrimination and indifference on the part of planning and implementation authorities as well as lack of awareness and knowledge of such schemes among Muslims. Consequently, the limited progress that some sections of Muslims have been able to make in recent years owes almost wholly to their own efforts. Overall the economic conditions of most Indian Muslims are unenviable, to say the least.

Most of them eke out a hand-to-mouth existence either by way of self-employment in petty trade or by working in the unorganized sector. They are engaged mostly as construction labourers, rickshaw, taxi and truck drivers, handcart pullers, coolies, barbers, tailors, carpenters, pavement hawkers, or at best as mechanics, fitters, plumbers, electricians or welders.
Also credit extended to them is very low.

Literacy Level by Religion and Gender (Census of India, 2001)

Religion	Male	Female	Total
Hindu	76.16	53.21	65.09
Muslim	67.66	50.09	59.13
Christian	84.37	76.19	80.25
Sikh	75.23	63.09	69.45
Buddhist	83.13	61.69	72.66
Jain	97.41	90.58	94.08

Political Representation:

There is a heavy decline in the Muslim representation in the Parliament and legislative assemblies.

The representation of Muslims in jobs is also very poor, the more we go up the ladder the representation comes down.

Successful Muslim Candidates in Civil Service Examinations

Year	Total	Selected Candidates	Muslims
1995-96	638	22	-
1999	Not Available	15	-
2001	417	12	-
2003	431	11	-
2005	422	08	-

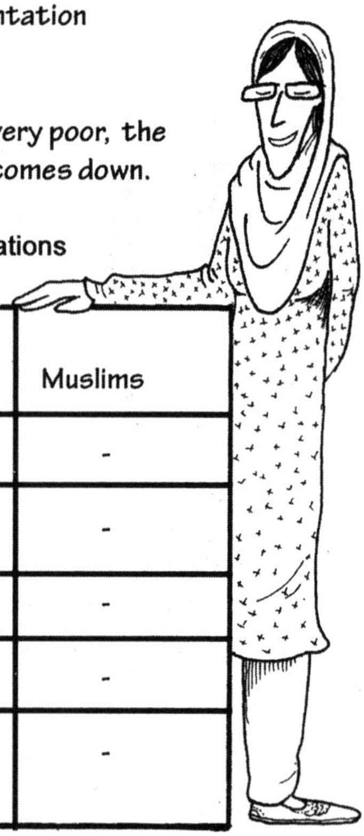

Source: Khalidi, Omar. 2006:46, Muslims in the Indian Economy, New Delhi: Three Essays Collective

The rate of population rise is higher amongst Muslims, they marry four times and shortly their population will overshoot the population of Hindus and this country will become a Muslim state.

The dominant communal forces over the years have propagated these myths. The communalists have on purpose projected the fear of Muslim population growth to consolidate their own electoral majority and towards this strategy they have effectively combined half-truths, ideological concoctions and rumour spreading techniques to entrench these myths in popular psyche.

We will like to begin with the myth that the rise in Muslim population is tremendously high and so they will outnumber the Hindus. The census surveys by religion totally negate this firmly held popular belief. Religion is one of the markers used in these surveys. As per 1971 survey, Hindus constituted 82.7 per cent and Muslims 11.2 per cent of the population. The corresponding figures for 1991 census are Hindus, 82.6 per cent and Muslims 11.4 per cent and for 2001, 80.5 per cent and 13.4 per cent respectively. (Malayalam Manorama, 1992). The 1991 data of Muslims does not include the data of Kashmir so the rise from 11.2 per cent to 13.4 per cent as large sections of Kashmiri Muslims was left out from the 1991 data. At the time of Partition the Muslim population was 11.6 per cent. Even in the current data there are some holes.

To begin with many an Adivasis have now got themselves registered in the category, 'other religions', rather than the previous Hindu which was automatically put in front of their names. This time Jains have also been put as a separate category so this decline in the rate of rise of Hindu population is not as big as it appears.

As such one is also amazed by the correlation of the population and religion. The rise of population is more an index of poverty and lack of education rather than the teachings of any religion. And no religious community is uniform all over India. The population growth rate amongst Kerala Muslims is very low compared to Muslims in other parts of the country. As Muslims have been a discriminated against a lot, their overall rate of population growth is higher. As awareness is spreading it is coming down uniformly. As such last two decades in particular have seen an increased intimidation and ghettoisation of Muslim community due to the communal violence, the worst of which was seen first in Mumbai riots in 1992-93 and in Gujarat in 2002. In such an adverse situation the social reforms and progress take a back seat. The need is to provide an atmosphere, where the community can live the social and political life with security and dignity.

That apart, even if the current differentials persist, it is not only unlikely, but impossible for Muslim population to overtake the Hindu population for the next century or so. On the contrary if the prevailing growth rates are analysed, it will be clear that between 61-71 and 71-81, Hindu population increase went up from 23.71 to 24.42, while between the same period Muslim population increase went down from 30.85 to 30.20. If these rate of growths are frozen at same level hundred years from 1981, Hindus and Muslims will record a decadal growth rate of 30.71 and 30.55 respectively i.e. growth rates of Hindus will be higher.

POLYGAMY (%) IN
INDIAN
POPULATION

(1961 CENSUS REPORT)

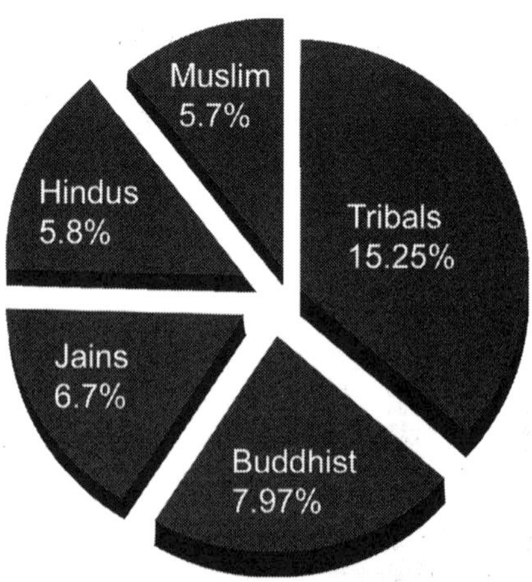

MYTH

Muslims do not practice family planning because of their religion.

FACT

It is true that a section of Islamic fundamentalist clergy does pass occasional fatwas to disapprove family planning, but a section of clergy can neither be equated to Islam, nor to Quran, nor to emerging Islamic practices as such. On the contrary many Ulemas of different countries have actually favoured temporary forms of family planning.

In his book 'Family planning and legacy of Islam', Islamic scholar A R Omran of Cairo dispels the myth that Islam is inherently against family planning. As per him there is no text in Koran prohibiting prevention of pregnancy. In Islamic countries like Turkey and Indonesia family planning methods are quite popular.

In Turkey, for example 63% of the population in the reproductive age group uses contraception and in Indonesia, the figure is 48%.
In India the number of Muslim couples in the child bearing age practising family planning in 1970 was 9%(Hindus 14%) and in 1980, 22.5%(Hindus 36.1%) (Operation Research Group: Baroda 1981)

Thus the number of additional Muslims taking to family planning is keeping pace with the number of Hindus doing the same. Like all other social programmes family planning is also linked with socio-economic status, level of general social awareness, etc. We will be repeatedly encountering this fact that a large number of Muslims being in the low socio-economic strata, share these statistics more with other socially disadvantaged sections of society.

MUSLIM FERTILITY FALL SHARPER THAN REST

The Sachar Committee report on the Muslim community has nailed the lie on the issue of Muslim reproduction and the "prevailing Muslim conspiracy" to reduce Hindus to minority status. The report, quoting extensively from Census reports and the National Health Survey, highlights how the last decade has witnessed a sharp decline in Muslim fertility rates as against the rest of the population. Estimates show that the total fertility rate (TFR) among Muslims declined from about 4.3 to 3.6 in the 1990s, a reduction of about 0.9 points.

During the same period fertility rates for the population as a whole declined from about 3.4 to 2.9, a reduction of nearly 0.5 points. The decline in fertility among Muslims was, therefore, sharper than average. Dr Rakesh Basak, an economist with IIM, Ahmedabad and a member of the committee, points out that at present "there is (only) a 0.7-point difference between the Muslim and the average fertility rate. While the average fertility rate is 2.9, for Muslims it is 3.6." Dr Basak emphasises that 37 per cent of Muslims use contraceptives against a national average of 48 per cent. Therefore, contraceptive usage is about 10 percentage points lower among Muslims than the average. However, there are significant regional variations. The use of contraceptives amongst Muslims is more widespread in Madhya Pradesh and Chhattisgarh than amongst Hindus in these states. In Gujarat, there is hardly any difference in the use of contraceptives across religious communities. In general, the report observes, contraceptive usage goes up with education and development and all communities benefit from such changes.

Of course, the availability of various contraceptive options also plays a major role in enhancing contraceptive use. Dr Basak says, "Data shows that on an average Muslims prefer using reversible methods of family planning as compared to nasbandi (sterilisation). This is true of several Hindu communities as well." He adds, "If there are severe supply-side constraints in the availability of the preferred contraceptive options, adoption may suffer. There is evidence to suggest that the unmet needs of the Muslim population for reversible methods of family planning are high." ..

(Asian Age 19/2/07)

Muslims often have more than one wife

The myth of polygamy amongst the Muslims is also very firmly rooted in popular mind. The correlation of polygamy with increase in population is the most simplistic concoction to have taken grip of our psyche. Overall the number of children born depends on the number of women in the reproductive age group and is limited by that.

On first count it is immaterial whether a man is having one or more wives as the total number of children depends on the number of women, which does not get influenced by polygamy. If at all, this number of women has more to do with the prevalence of social practice of female infanticide and 'bride burnings' in the areas where the practice of extortion by parents of 'grooms' called dowry is prevalent. Secondly, the male/female ratio can not permit the 'luxury' of four wives to the Muslim males unless three-fourths (75%) of them go without marriage. As per 2001 census the male/female ratio for Muslims was 936 and for Hindus 931 i.e., for every 1000 Muslim males there are 936 Muslim females. One has to conceive of gigantic mental acrobatics, in the light of these statistics, to believe that all Muslim males can have four wives.

As such a slightly earlier but relevant statistics of polygamy (1961 census report) totally smashes the myth of Muslim polygamy, unless the social trends have worsened drastically, which obviously have not. As per this the incidence of polygamy is highest percentage among the Adivasis (15.25) followed by Buddhists (7.9), Jains (6.72) Hindus (5.80) and lo behold, followed by Muslims (5.70). Research carried out by Mallika B.Mistry of Gokhle institute of Pune, concludes "there is no evidence that the percentage of polygamous marriage (among Muslims) is larger than for Hindus". (1998) A comparison of nuptiality patterns for Hindus and Muslims shows great similarity,the incidence of polygamy has been declining among both Hindus and Muslims.

From the above, it will be interesting to draw the religion based fertility patterns. These patterns differ within Muslim community itself, they vary from region to region as per the socio-economic and educational levels of the community concerned. Those in the better socio-economic and educational ladder have lesser population increase, while those on the lower rungs of socio-economic educational ladder have higher rate of population growth. This conforms to regional, urban and rural distribution as well. Birth rates in Malabar region of Kerala, whose Muslim population is 40%, is significantly lower than those in Uttar Pradesh with a Muslim population of 15%. The contrasting case is that of Kashmir, a Muslim majority state. Here the fertility rate of Hindus is almost twice that of Muslims. Here again the birth rate was lower 31.4(per thousand) than in U.P (36.5), MP (36.4), Bihar (34.8) and Rajasthan (33.4).

Can we bother to realise that the overall rate of population increase in educationally and socially advanced states like Kerala, Tamilnadu and Karnataka, is lower, both for Muslims and Hindus, compared to the rest of the country. Also let us have a look at Urban rural divide. More than one-third of the Muslim community is concentrated in the peripheral and decaying areas of urban economic life. Incidence of urban poverty is higher among them by 17% (vis-a-vis Hindus). The number of Muslims living below poverty line is close to 44% (National figure-28%). They are generally living in older areas of modern cities, which are well known for poor sanitation, lack of health facilities and basic amenities. On the top of this the repeated outburst of communal violence against them is 'ghettoising' them with the result that improvement in their lot is becoming more and more difficult.

Overall, one observes that there are multiple factors determining the rate of population growth, religion being very low on weight-age scale, if at all it counts. Socio-economic betterment and education are the foremost factors helping in the control of population growth. Feeling of insecurity and poor socio-economic status counter the efforts to promote family planning, (nee, welfare, which is the term conveying the goals of this exercise more precisely), and these two factors transcend the religious factor by a number of times. In such a complex scenario, the propaganda machine of the Sangh Parivar has done a 'remarkable job by making' Ham do, hamare do: Woh panch, unke pachees (We (Hindus) practise two children norm, they (Muslims) practise four wives, twenty five children norm), a part of social common sense'. One has to 'complement' the Gobbelsian methods of Hindu right, which have concocted this offensive slogan, which is far removed from the truth.

CHRISTIAN

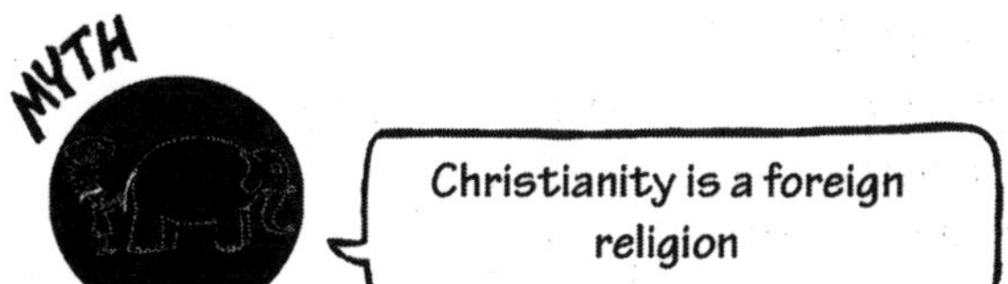

Right during first century A.D. Christianity entered India through the trading ships from the West. Legend of St. Thomas has been associated with coming of Christianity to India, as he came twice on a mission to India. His second mission, for which there is stronger evidence, was around 52 A.D. to Malabar Coast. He established a series of Syrian churches along the coast.

The angry local people who are opposed to the forced conversions being done by the Christians are attacking Christians

The attacks on Christians have begun especially from last 1997 onwards. These attacks are being orchestrated by different organizations linked to RC and a general hysteria is being created against the Christian Missionaries in particular.

During this year (1998-99) many a priests were humiliated (Fr. Christudas being paraded naked in Dumka), one of them being burnt alive along with his two sons aged 9 and 7, many a churches have been damaged in these attacks, Bibles have been burnt and nuns have been raped in interior places. This has occurred in the backdrop of anti-Christian propaganda as per which Christianity is a foreign religion, their missionary activities are a mere ploy for inducing people for conversions to adopt Christianity; their schools and hospitals are mere tools for the same. The CIA is planning this process and the Pope and Christian agencies, which are out to evangelize the whole country, whereby Hindus will become a minority.
Most of the inquiries by social activists, National Human Rights Commission, National Minorities Commission have shown that different organisations affiliated to SP are behind these attacks, and the attacks are taking place mostly in the BJP ruled states, Gujarat in particular.

Christian missionaries have been setting up Churches, seminaries and schools wherever and whenever possible. They learnt Indian Languages, set up printing presses and published religious as well as secular literature, to spread literacy and their faith. In the process they adopted Indian languages for their communication and the Church adopted a number of native practices. Despite 2000 years of Christian presence, and 200 years of British rule the population of Christians in 1971 was 2.6 %, which in 1981 stood at 2.44%, in 1991 it was 2.32 and in 2001 it is 2.3%.

Despite this the threat of 'their' population overtaking the Hindu population has begun only from one year or so.
This anti-Christian bogey comes at a time when the anti-Muslim pogroms have more or less 'achieved the target' of permanently intimidating and ghettoizing them. Also SP realizes that if it has to break the electoral jinx to be able to come to power on its own, it needs a newer vote bank and for this adivasis have been seen as ones having the best potential.

There is also a growing realization in RC that after conversion to Christianity the adivasis have become more educated and aware of their rights, and this is a big threat to 'status quo', which is the baseline of politics. These two factors seem to be the major ones in the current strategy of intimidating the missionaries. The calculation is that after this type of 'treatment' they will be reluctant to go to the remote places and that will make the job of wooing Adivasis to its fold comparatively easy.

Letter of a Woman BJP functionary (Mrs. Philomina) who resigned from BJP to Mr. Yediyurappa BJP Karnataka President, in the wake of attacks on Christians

APPENDIX-1

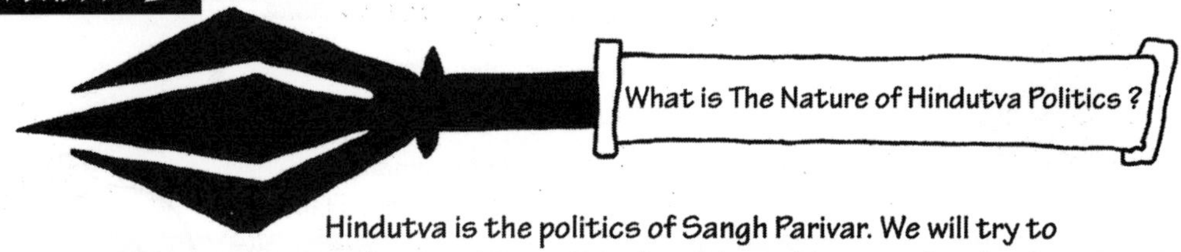

Hindutva is the politics of Sangh Parivar. We will try to understand its political nature and its social and political goals.

Hindutva is the new name for Hinduism

This is not true. As we will see Hinduism is a religion while Hindutva is the politics of a section of society, which wants to dominate the social scene for its political and social interests.

Hinduism	Hindutva
A collation of multiple traditions: Brahminism- Shramanism- Tantra, Kabir, Tukaram	Politics of Hindu elite, drawing from Brahminical Hinduism.
Brahminism: Caste system, the dominant ethos	Brew of Brahminical Hinduism and Nationalism
Brahminism projected as Hinduism initially in 6-10 century, then in early 19th century, Brahminical Hinduism projected to be synonymous with Hinduism.	Aims at Hindu Rashtra based on Brahminical Hinduism
Shramanic traditions: Constant rebellion: attempt to escape the clutches of Brahminism: Conversion to Buddhism (early times and now after the lead given by Ambedkar). Leadership from upper caste.	Led initially by Brahmins: Banias even now dominant
'Dharma' is a mix of Humanism and caste based religious duties.	Political expression through sangh parivar now, earlier Hindu mahasabha and RSS.
Semitisation process being spearheaded by Sangh Parivar. Attempt to set up monolithic unity with holy deity: Ram, Holy Book: Gita clergy: Shankaracharyas etc.	A mix of fundamentalism and Fascism.
Its proponents claim it to be tolerant and catholic.	VHP brings in the stink of fundamentalism in the essentially fascist politics of RSS, BJP and Bajrangdal.

If Hindutva is not religion then what is it?

As pointed out above it is a political phenomenon. It has characteristics, which are a mix of Fundamentalism and Fascism both. It is a peculiar phenomenon, and has its own peculiarities which fall in neither of these categories,

COMPARING HINDUTVA AND FUNDAMENTALISM	
HINDUTVA	FUNDAMENTALISM
Targeting against liberal ethos of the society.	Same
Imposition of retrograde social values selectively culled out from religious texts.	Same
Swadeshi is the 'economic policy'	Anti imperialist noises
Built around (Gita, Vedas), Ram and Acharyas	Based on Semitic religion-Holy book, Holy daily and clergy
Harping on traditional orthodox beliefs	Same
Projection of women as ideal mothers	Women under patriarchal control of father, husband and son
Claims that Vedas are created by Brahma	Claim that 'Our' creed based on divine law: holy book coming from God himself
Golden past of religious rule is shown to be the ideal goal	Same
Demands homogeneity of Hindu culture political onslaught to impose interest of elite, middle classes and upper caste and the whole of society	Abhor pluralism. Creates hysteria (against Shah of Iran, in Iran, against women in Saudi Arabia)
Creates hysteria against internal enemy, the Muslim	Hysteria against Women, Imperialism, neighboring country
Great importance to women's dress code	Same
Built around emotive appeal of religion	Same

SIMILARITIES AND DIFFERENCES BETWEEN HINDUTVA AND FASCISM

HINDUTVA

FASCISM

HINDUTVA	FASCISM
SIMILARITIES	
(1) It got strengthened in post-Mandal period: after fearing the assertion of lower castes.	Came up and became strong in the wake of powerful workers movement
(2) Projects 'National' interests over the interests of the people.	Same
(3) Has the seeds of expansionism; concept of 'Akhand Bharat' (undivided India, including Pakistan, Myanmar, Bangladesh and Sri Lanka)	Expansionist: attacked neighbouring Countries on the ground that they were part of earlier German empire
(4) Targeting Muslims as the cause of the ills of the country	Targeting Jews as the cause of ills of the country.
(5) Glorification of the past.	Same
(6) Oppressive to workers (produce for nation, don't bother about your Rights), Dalits (oppose Mandal in a subtle way of demand for meritocracy), women (they should be ideal wives and mothers), minorities (they should subjugate themselves to Hindu culture).	Oppressive to Jews, (subjected them to physical elimination), Communists/workers (physical violence to reduce their strength), women (their place is in the kitchen, church and their primary role is in rearing children).
(7) Post Babri demolition resulted in social space full of terror and anti-human rights, 'pro'-national hysteria.	The regime implemented its pogrom through creation of mass hysteria.
(8) Urbanised middle class and rich peasants/upper castes and some backward castes: the main support base.	Urban middle class and landed Aristocracy: the main social base.
Differences	
(1) Long gestation period: successful communalisation of social space in 'cowbelt' region; success in polarisation of upper castes only after implementation of Mandal Commission.	Quick ascendancy to power on the anti Jew plank.
(2) Medium range social crisis from mid 80's : rising unemployment, increasing poverty.	Severe post World War economic crisis.

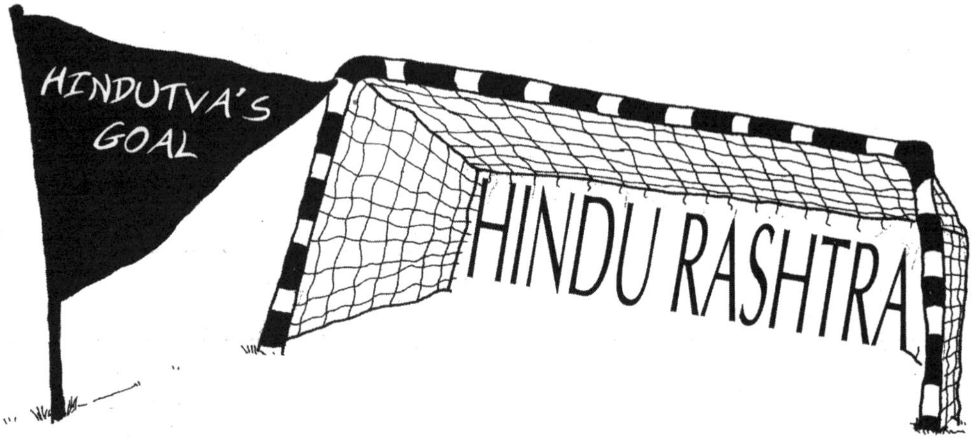

Hindu Rashtra is not a religious state; it is a `modern phenomenon to impose the pre-modern social hierarchies on all sections of society. It is the goal of a section of society, which is the major beneficiary of current social privileges, the section of society, which has gained in the process of development of last few decades.

It was the goal of a section of society which was threatened by the social changes in pre-independence times (Zamindar-Brahmins) and who were champions of status quo and were allies of British at economic and political level. The Hindu Rashtra which is threatening to engulf the society from last two decades is the battle cry of sections who again are upholder of a status quo vis-a-vis social position of women, workers, dalits and adivasis.

It is the offence of a section of society, which has benefited maximum by proliferation of small industries, petty business and agriculture of the `Green Revolution' type.

Indian Nationalism as an encompassing concept based itself on secular grounds and attempts to strive for formal liberty, equality and fraternity; supplemented by the liberal space to struggle to convert these formal concepts in to reality. Indian Nationalism is a positive concept, incorporating different religions, ethnicities and cultures and is an integral part of world economy and emerging global village.

The slow speed of this movement has its inherent problems. Whereas on one hand it can capture the social space, on the other it can also elicit a reaction to itself. This reaction to it from Dalits, workers, women, section of middle class that is secular, is a big obstacle to the march of Hindutva. The major industrial houses have a unique relation with Sangh Parivar. Whenever faced with crisis to their own existences, the socially terrorising atmosphere created by Sangh Parivar helps the bourgeoisie to wriggle out of the compulsions of liberal ethos. The conservative movement of Sangh Parivar helps the needs of capital to keep thriving in an uninterrupted way.

Thus this chronic, resilient, thriving Fascism, expressed through the vehicle of Sangh Parivar continues to throw up different shades of its existence, sometimes terrorizing (to the poor and the minorities) sometimes aggressive (to the neighbouring `enemy' countries), and sometimes even appearing to collapse under the weight of its own contradictions. But the march, at the moment is on. The social roots of Hindutva are all for the support and continuation of the repressive capitalist regime; sustaining the bourgeoisie aspirations, while continuing to pursue its own project.

Hindutva onslaught draws some support from fundamentalist concepts also. It calls out from the past-selective values to impose them on present. It uses religious imagery, glorifies the `golden past' of rule of Hindu kings, sees women primarily under patriarchal control dictating their way of life, dress code, etc. It co-opts all the sundry religious professionals and personnels to strengthen its political base and it uses religion in a very effective way to create the nationalist hysteria.

At present the situation is fairly in balance. The onslaught has achieved mammoth proportions in the north, but south and east are comparatively unaffected by its paranoid aggression. The reaction of Dalits, though fragmented is definitely going to retard the march of the *'rath'* (Chariot) of Hindutva.

The apparent target of Sangh Parivar, the Muslims, are in a bind. On one hand they have been battered so much by Hindutva that they cannot afford to lie quiet any more. Secondly unlike the Dalits they lie in sub-critical zone of backwardness where they find it difficult to come out of the grip of their own `religious leaders', `the Muslim obscurantists' posing to be speaking on behalf of their community. Thus they face a double attack from both Hindu Fascism and Muslim fundamentalism.

Probably the suffering of the `poor Muslims' is so great they will be forced to come out and resist the `bear's hug' of Sangh Parivar and by side-tracking their `obscurantist leaders' will pose definite obstacle to the march of `Trishuls (Tridents) of Hindutva'. How Sangh Parivar overcomes this 'problem' which new `velvet gloves' it discovers to remove this obstacle remains to be seen.

TASKS FOR SECULAR MOVEMENT

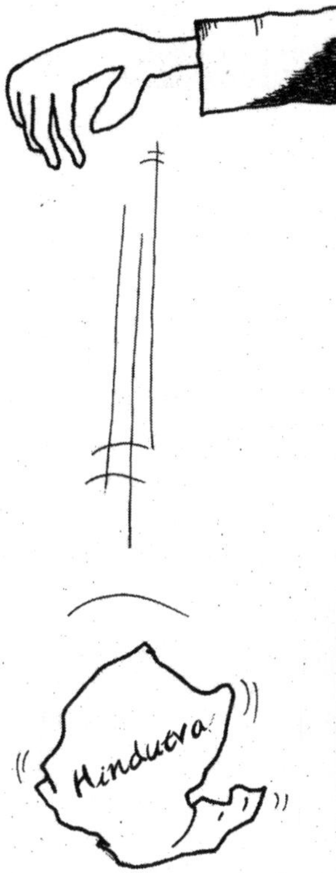

With growth of autonomous movements each struggling sector is asserting itself through small attempts to work for, to wrest its rights. This is a non-hegemonic way of struggle of the oppressed. Unfortunately this has a potential of advancement in liberal atmosphere only, where these fragmented, isolated struggles and movements can stand on their own feet to march towards their goals.

Hindutva is succeeding in creating a social atmosphere, where it will be difficult for these struggles to be carried on properly. Already numerous hurdles are cropping up in the march of these movements. These movements share anti-authoritarianism, which can be the basis of their coming together, to combat Hindutva, despite their seemingly diverse social agendas.

The common platform, which coordinates, without suppressing the aspirations of individual constituents, can aim against the Fascist Hindutva and strengthen the secular, democratic rights of large sections of society. That alone can form the basis of secular, democratic ethos, which can stand against the onslaught of Hindutva and in the long-term show it, its place in the history, the dustbin.

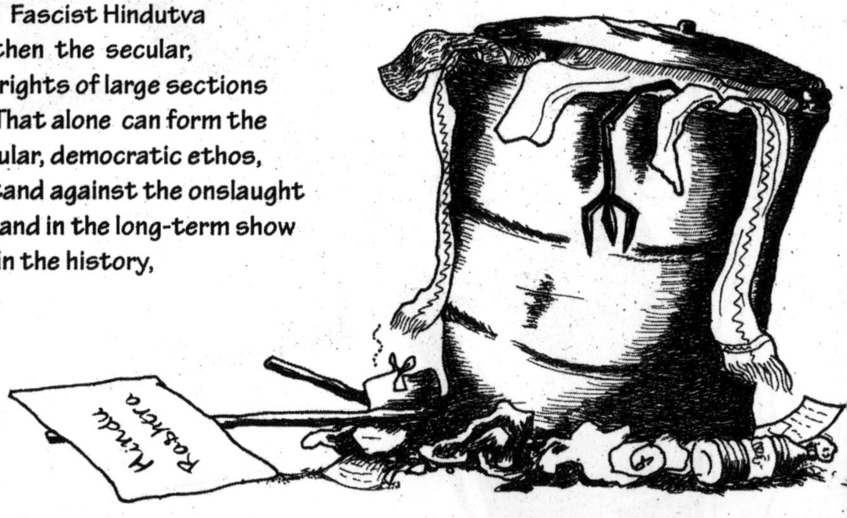

APPENDIX-2

HINDUTVA POLITICS : HISTORICAL GENESIS

The terms Hindus and Hinduism are Orientalist 'constructions' originating in late 18th century, promoted by the British administrators who believed 'The essence of India existed in a number of key Hindu classical scriptures such as the Vedas, the codes of Manu and the Shastras that often prescribe hierarchical ideas, a conclusion eagerly supported and elaborated by Brahmins". (Hyness Doughlas & Gyan Prakash (eds) 1991)

This fabrication through repetition of "India as unitary Hindu Society has obscured the reality of segmented society with Brahmins and other upper castes exercising a monopoly of power, fabricated Hinduism is found everywhere" (Arthur Bonner: 1994).

Romila Thapar (1987) summarises the whole process very succinctly, The new Hinduism which is being currently propagated by sanghs, parishads and samajas is an attempt to restructure the indigenous religions as a monolithic uniform religion rather paralleling some of the features of semitic religions.

This seems to be a fundamental departure from the essentials of what may be called the indigenous Hindu religions. Its form is not only in many ways alien to the earlier culture of India, but equally disturbing is the uniformity which it seeks to impose on the variety of Hindu religions.

Hinduism as defined in the contemporary parlance, is a collation of beliefs, rites and practices consciously selected from the past, interpreted in contemporary idiom in last couple of centuries and the selection conditioned by historical circumstances in a strict sense. A reference to Hinduism would require a more precise definition of a particular variety Brahmo Samaj, Arya Samaj, shaiva, siddhanta, bhakti, tantricism or whatever.

This process of construction of Hinduism occurred in two periods, one in the period spanning from 6th to 10th century. The second phase is still on, starting from the periods of Arya Samaj, Hindu Sabha (Punjab) Hindu Mahasabha (from 1915) and finally with RSS (1925) and its progeny, VHP (from 1960s).

Initially Hinduism was vaguely being made the base of the politics of the Hindu elite and revivalists. With return of Savarkar from Andamans a new and more focussed political Hinduism emerged. Savarkar's work 'Hindutva: Who is a Hindu" (1923) became and remains the basic text defining this political concept. Savarkar argued (later on this became the ideological base of most of the Hindutva organisations) the Aryans who settled in India at the dawn of history already formed a nation, now embodied in the Hindus ...... Hindus are bound together not only by the tie of the love they bear to a common fatherland and by the common blood that courses through their veins and keeps our hearts throbbing and our affection warm but also by the tie of the common homage we pay to our great civilization, our Hindu culture (Savarkar; 1923)

Thus "Hindutva according to him rests on three pillars: geographical unity, racial features and common culture." (Christophe Jaffrelot, 1993). He further went on to elaborate the criterion for who is a Hindu? According to him, all those who regard this land as their fatherland and holy land are the only ones who are Hindu and thereby the people to whom this land belongs.

This led to the automatic interpretations that the Christians and the Muslims, whose holy places are in Jerusalem and Mecca are not on par with the Hindus who own this country. Initiating the theorising of the doubting of patriotism of Muslims, Savarkar posits, but besides culture the tie of common holy land has at times proved stronger than the chains of a motherland.

Look at Mohammedans: Mecca to them is a sterner reality than Delhi or Agra (Savarkar, 1923). This development of the concept of Hindutva comes in succession to the construction of Brahminism as Hinduism and this Brahminical Hinduism then forming the base for Hindutva politics. Savarkar began to articulate the ideology of Hindu elite (zamindars, brahmins, kings) by integrating Brahminical Hinduism with nationalism, calling it Hindutva which further showed the way for building the Hindu Rashtra. His key sentence was "Hinduise all politics and militarize all Hindudom".

These concepts were further refined and given the parallel projection by M. S. Golwalkar, the second supremo (Sarsanghchalak) of RSS, an organisation formed in 1925, ostensibly aimed to train young boys in "Hindu Culture". Its ideology was based on Brahminical Hinduism; Hindutva and it aspired for the formation of Hindu Rashtra.

This body which began as exclusively upper caste Hindu male organisation (and continues to be so despite some sprinkling of low castes and a rare show piece in the form of a Muslim or a Christian) concentrated in indoctrinating adolescent boys in the 'hate other' (Muslim) ideology and began slowly consolidating in different parts of cow belt to begin with. Golwalkar drawing heavily from Nazi ideology went on to elaborate the ideas on Nation, Hindu Rashtra, in his book 'We or our Nationhood defined' and 'Bunch of Thoughts'.

He was forthright in his criticism of Nationalism of Congress, and its 'amazing' theory "that the nation is composed of all those who for one reason or the other happen to live at the time in a country" (Golwalkar, 1968). For Golwalkar racial factor in nationhood is crucial and he goes on to propound, "To keep up the purity of Race and its culture, Germany shocked the world by her purging the country of Semitic races, the Jews".

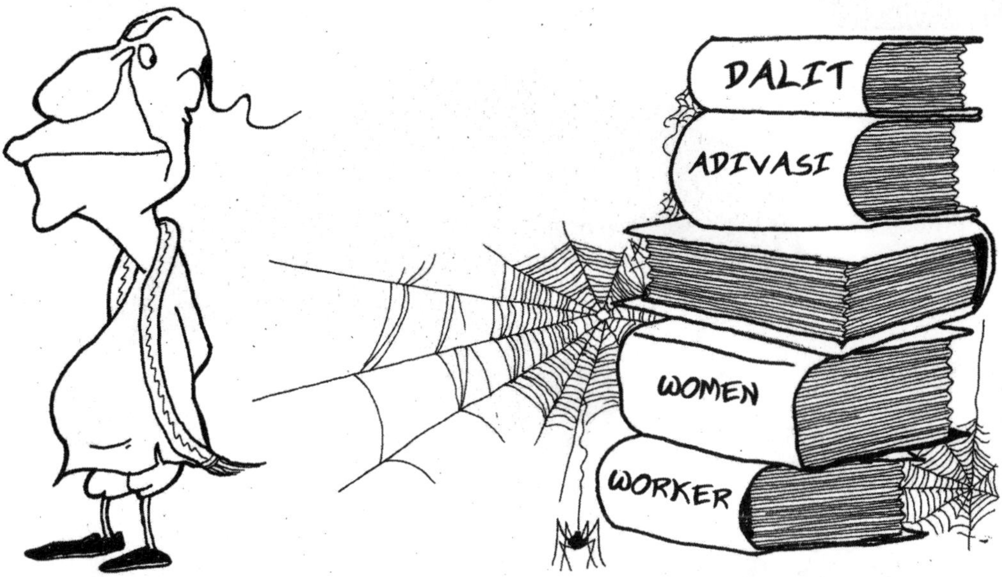

Race pride at its highest has been manifested here. Germany has also shown how well nigh impossible it is for races and cultures having differences going to the root, to be assimilated into one united whole, a good lesson for us in Hindustan to learn and profit by. (Golwalkar, 1938). He is very candid in showing the other races and those belonging to 'foreign' religions their place, 'The foreign races in Hindustan must either adopt the Hindu culture and language, must learn to respect and hold in reverence Hindu religion, must entertain no ideas but those of glorification of the Hindu race and culture or may stay in the country wholly subordinated to the Hindu nation claiming nothing, deserving no privileges, far less any preferential treatment not even citizens rights." (Golwalkar, 1938).

It was the goal of a section of society which was threatened by the social changes in pre independence times (Zamindar-Brahmins) and those who were champions of status quo and were allies of British at economic and political level. The Hindu Rashtra which is threatening to engulf the society from last two decades is the battle cry of a section of society who again are upholder of a status quo vis-a-vis social position of women, workers, dalits and adivasis. It is the offense of this section of society which has benefited maximum by proliferation of small industries, petty business and agriculture of the 'Green revolution' type.

APPENDIX-3

VANDE MATRAM CONTROVERSY

After Arjun Singh, HRD Minister clarified that singing of the (August 2006) Vande Matram is voluntary, on 7th September, the supposed centenary year of this song, BJP went hammer and tongs blaming Congress for this 'appeasement' of minorities. In the meanwhile, a section of Muslims had protested that the song is asking for worship of deities other than Allah, and that is something, which Islam does not permit. One could see the charged BJP members shouting Vande Matram in the upper house of the parliament, led by Mukhtar Abbas Naqvi. Various Hindutva ideologues gave a threat that those who do not want to sing this song should leave the country. BJP is planning to sing the song in its party head offices on that day. Chattisgarh has already issued the circular to all the schools, including the madarsas to sing this song on that day, and other BJP ruled states, MP, Gujarat, and Rajasthan are on the way to issue the same.

A section of Muslim clerics including Shahi Imam of Jama Masjid, have raised objection to it saying that Islam being monotheistic does not regard any other object as god or goddess but all Muslims have not opposed it. Surely A. R. Rahman, the music maestro has got this song into a beautiful catchy and popular tune. Shahi Imam, who has opposed the move, has been very close to BJP and has been repeatedly wooed by this party for electoral purposes to the extent that in the last Lok Sabha elections, he went to issue the Fatwa for the Muslims to vote for BJP.

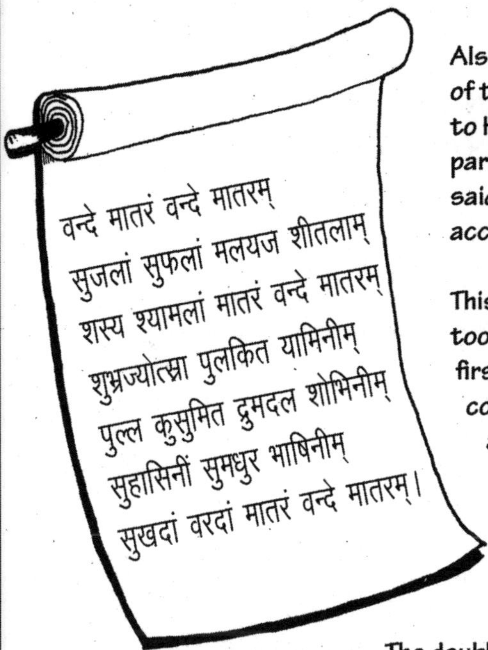

Also it should be clear that the later parts of the song where the motherland is compared to Hindu goddesses was not accepted as the part of national song, by the committee which said that only first two stanzas should be accepted as national song.

This is what constitutional position is, and that too it was made clear that the singing of the first two stanzas of the song is voluntary, not a compulsory one. There is a reasonable deal of argument not to accept to sing the full song by a section of Muslim population due to its Hindu imagery.

The double standards of Hindutva lobby are very clear in this controversy. In 1998, when UP Govt wanted to make it compulsory the then Prime minister, Mr. Vajpayee opined against this move of UP Government.

RSS and the Hindutva family are strongly hung up on this song, more so than the Jana Gana Mana, the national anthem. After writing the first two stanzas of Vande Matram, Bankim Chandra Chatterjee expanded it in his novel Anand Math. Large part of it is in Sanskrit, Devbhasha, and few stanzas are in Bengalee. The song was sung by anti British protestors and it also has pro Hindu overtones. A section of secular movement resorted to it during its anti British campaigns, while Hindutva sections upheld it for the Hindu undertones and they used it as a battle cry against the Muslims in the communal violence, who in turn resorted to Allah-o-Akbar. It matched with the requirements of Hindutva movement as here the nation is projected as a monolithic being, in the image of Durga. Jana Gana Mana, Vande matram and Saare Jahan Se Achchha were the three national songs in the running for the national anthem. Jana Gana Mana conveyed the rich diversity and was acceptable to most states, due to which it was selected as national anthem while Vande Matram, first two stanzas, was given the status of national song. RSS family is using it to browbeat the minorities. Here it does not matter that even the national anthem cannot be imposed on those who do not wish to sing that, as per the judgment of the court. But surely for BJP, which is built around the identity issues, Ram Temple, Cow, Civil code etc. it is a golden opportunity.

Jana Gana Mana, which is more acceptable to all, is purposely pushed back by these elements. They are projecting it as having been written by Rabindranath Tagore in praise of *George V*. This myth was created by the English media. In 1911 when *George V* visited India, Congress wanted to thank him for retracting the British decision to partition Bengal. This was the first success of Swadeshi movement, the first modern anti colonial movement, which had begun in 1905. On the same day two songs were sung, one written by Tagore, Jana Gana Mana and the other that of one Ramanuj Choudhary, who had composed the song especially for *George V*. The English media was neither accurate nor serious about properly reporting such events. So what got reported by the British media was that Tagore's song was sung in praise of *George V*!

When Tagore was asked by a friend, who was loyal to British, to write a song in praise of *George V*, Tagore felt angered as he was opposed to the British rule. Instead of one for *George* he wrote a song devoted to the dispenser of human destiny. When faced with British media projection and RSS type criticism, Tagore wrote "That great Charioteer of man's destiny in age after age could not by any means be *George V* or *George VI* or any *George*. Even my 'loyal' friend realized this; because, however powerful his loyalty to the King, he was not wanting in intelligence." The song gained wide popularity all over and its English translation, 'Morning song of India' also picked in different parts. Netaji's Azad Hind Fauz adopted it as national anthem and Gandhiji went on to say, "the song has found a place in our national life." It is precisely for this reason that RSS affiliates are uncomfortable with Jana Gana Mana and want to assert Vande Matram in an aggressive way.

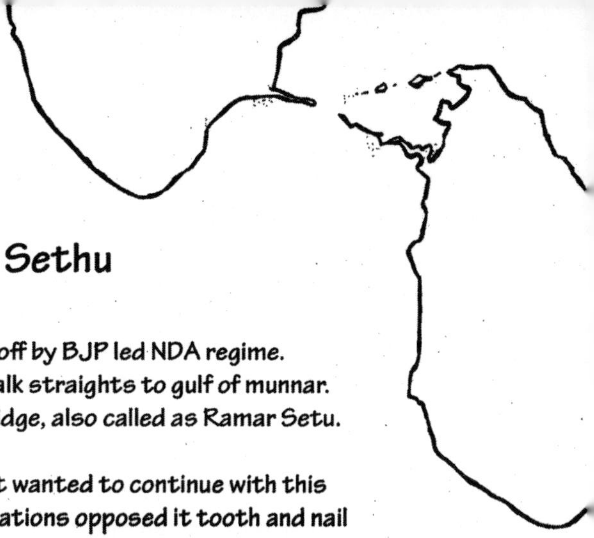

Adam Bridge or Ram Sethu

Setusamudram Project was set off by BJP led NDA regime. This aims to make a canal from Palk straights to gulf of munnar. It involved dredging of Adams Bridge, also called as Ramar Setu.

Later when Cogress led UPA Govt wanted to continue with this project, BJP and affiliate organizations opposed it tooth and nail as planned. The argument now is that this project will destroy Ramar Setu, the one which was built by Vanar Sena (Army of Monkeys) to help Ram cross over to Lanka to rescue Sita.

This project when complete, it will cut short the long journey of the ships from east coast to the west coast, and vice versa. Like Panama Canal it has been conceived to promote transport, employment and to improve trade. Half way now, it has been facing two oppositions. One is from the environmentalists, who are worried about the destruction of flora and fauna and the dangers of silting in the canal. These are the arguments which need to be taken seriously.

The other ground, the one based on faith need to be dealt with at another level. RSS and its affiliates are promoting a view that building this Sethusamudram will involve the destruction of Ramar Sethu which will be detrimental to our faith.

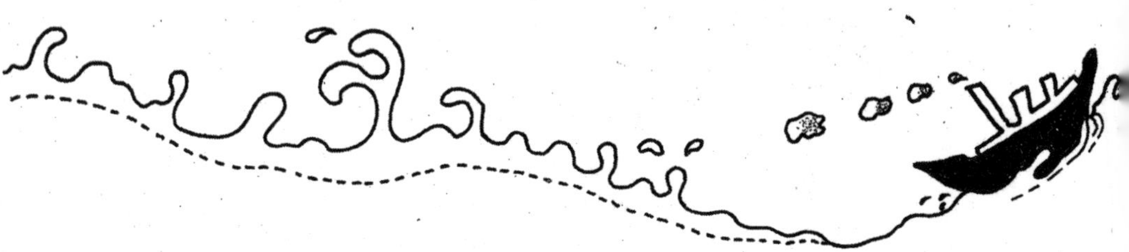

The story goes that Ravan, the King of Lanka had abducted Sita to avenge the insult meted out to his sister Shurpnakha, whose proposal for marrying her was turned down by Lord Ram. Assisted by his loyal devotee Hanuman, the Lord mobilized monkeys and built this bridge. It is claimed that this bridge is a marvel of engineering achievements of the Indian engineers of that time. The assertion is that it shows the acme of technological achievements of this land, and that there are other noteworthy achievements like the advances in aeronautical technologies like aeroplanes, missiles to name a few.

How do we understand these claims, how do we comprehend this peep into the past? How do we distinguish fact from fiction, history from mythology? To reconcile history, science and mythology are the complex questions in our public life. To begin with, history of events has some definitive characteristics, though their interpretations do vary with the political ideologies. But what about mythology? Here these accounts have been put forward as the fictional accounts of the past. Some of these accounts have been associated with faith. Faith to some extent is natural and sometimes it is being manufactured and asserted for political goals.

As far as Lord Ram's story goes there are several versions of Ramayana, (Many Ramayanas, Richman, OUP). Some of these are very popular like Valmiki Ramayana and Tulasidas Ramcharitmanas. Surely the most popular one currently is the one from Maharashi Ramanand Sagar's mega serial which captivated the nation for couple of years. There are other versions, which have been undermined and attacked mostly for political reasons. Sahmat exhibition on different versions of Lord Ram's story was attacked few years ago. Some politically motivated people could not bear one of the versions presented in this exhibition.

It showed that according to Jataka version of Ram-Katha, in post Brahminical Buddhist Dashrath Jataka Sita is both sister and wife of Ram. As per this version Dashrath is King not of Ayodhya but of Varanasi. The marriage of sister and brother is part of the tradition of glorious Kshatriya clans who wanted to maintain their caste and clan purity. This Jataka tale shows Ram to be the follower of Buddha. Similarly in Jain versions of Ramayana project Ram as the propagator of anti-Brahminical Jain values, especially as a follower of non-violence. What do both Buddhist and Jain versions have in common is that in these Ravan is not shown as a villain but a great soul dedicated to quest of knowledge and is a spiritual soul, with majestic commands over passions, a sage and a responsible ruler. Popular and prevalent 'Women's Ramayan Songs (of Telugu Brahmin Women), put together by Rangnyakmma, keep the women's concern as the central theme and present alternate perspective. These songs present Sita as finally victorious over Ram and in these Shurpnakha succeeds in taking revenge over Ram.

Prof. Victor Mannikam, of Satara University points out (Times of India, 14th Sept. 2007) that this epic dates back to 5000 years while Ramar Setu is over a lakh years old. Prof. V. S. Sahay of Anthropology Department of Allahabad University says that the society described in Ramayana represents Metal age (5000-6000 BC) and Ram's Vanar army has not constructed the structure as it belongs to Pleistocene age which shows emergence of stone tools. Marine experts tell us that the setu itself is a marine structure over a lakh years old and not man made. It is a natural occurence of the continuity of sandstone sedimentation which streches below Dhanushkoti and isotope dating indicates that the deposition is over a lakh years old (Prof. R. Mannikam).

Thus one can conclude that Ramar Setu is a much older structure, called tombol, a sand deposition due to natural process, connecting one land with another, and that it is from times when human habitation is doubtful. The Geological Survey of India has also ruled out its being a manmade (or monkey made!), construction. Same way the inference from NASA satellite pictures is that it is due to sedimentation of clay and limestone.

Many people dispute that the Lanka mentioned in Ramayana is not the current Sri Lanka. Since mythology does not require any proof it can be modulated and constructed into a faith for political purposes.

FAITH

Recently in the Shabri Kumbh held in Dang in Gujarat, the mythology was modulated in to the service of politics. It was said, and that too with great amount of precision, that a particular hillock, which was earlier called Chamak Dongar, which adivasis used to worship as Shivar Deo (protector of crops), was the precise place where Shabri had offered berries to Lord Ram. It was rechristened and a Shabri temple was built on the spot. Nearby, a river six kilometers away, Purna was named as the one where Guru Matang Rishi use to take bath.
On the mountain on a stone there were three marks which are being presented as the marks where Laxman had sharpened his arrows.

It is easy to construct a flyover to the future but difficult to prevent the formation of mythological bridges of the past. Mythology can easily be constructed and planted in the people's psyche as it is driven by political goals and rides on horse of emotion. Reason and logic have no place in this scheme of things. One knows that some Mullahs, having faith in the infinite power of djinns advocated their rulers to invest in the research for making more djinns so that power crisis can be solved. Further, with the resurgence of fundamentalism, one is hearing that 'Creation science' is back in the race to compete with the theories of evolution. The question is, should we misuse faith, faith which can be an assuaging balm, for building political agendas?

APPENDIX-5

TERRORISM

Roots of Terrorism

The argument that terrorists come from all religions and that it has nothing to do with the religions is being countered by another argument that there is something inherent in the teachings of Islam from which the current terrorists derive the legitimacy for their actions.

Some Muslim scholars and activists are also pointing out that we should not be in the denial mode and see the roots of such actions in our religious traditions when violence was permitted, resorted to in the face of attacks from those opposed to the rising Islam.

It is true that when Islam was coming up as a religion it was opposed by a section of tribes, who used to attack the new converts to Islam. In that context, as a measure of defence Prophet Mohammad pointed out that violence can be undertaken as a last resort if all other methods fail. One should also note that Islam, the word itself stands for peace. The core word of greetings of Muslims, Assalam Valekum, Salam means peace in Arabic. It is ironical that the religion which strove to bring the message of peace for mankind is being projected as the repository of violence and some of its own scholars are agreeing to this formulation.

As a religion is a multidimensional phenomenon; the major components of religions can be broadly classified as those falling in the categories of morality and identity. Morality pertains to the values of social relationship and ethical norms as embodied in those of Vasudhev Kutumbakam, (whole World is my family) Love thy neighbour, or ensure that your neighbour is also doing well. The identity part pertains more to the rituals, worship, reverence for holy books, belief in the supernatural and bowing to the authority of clergy, priesthood in different garbs. Surely the Kings who undertook crusades, jihads or dharmyuddhas were operating in the name of identity.

Even in other religions there is an invocation of religion, like Bush calling for crusade in the aftermath of 9/11, or Togadia calling the Gujarat carnage as the glory of Hindu religion. As far as violence is concerned there is hardly a religious tradition which may not have invoked the religion to undertake it or incite their soldiers to carry on with violence in that name. While Old Testament does talk of violence at places, Gita is elaborated as the philosophy mainly to ensure that Arjun, the hero of Mahabharat, takes the path of violence against his own cousins.

As far as intolerance is attributed to Islam, one recalls that tolerance and intolerance are parts of all religious traditions. Koran states, to you your faith, to me mine. Hinduism states, truth is one but there are many paths to reach it. In the same religion there are other parts which will invoke it to impose their norms on others.

When we see the fanatic, violent terrorists undertaking the bombing and talking of Islam, crusade, Jihad, an impression is created that there is something inherent in Islam.

Holy Koran

As far as Islam is concerned, while it does ask to resort to violence in self defence, at the same time it also instructs that the killing of even a single innocent is like killing the whole humanity and that saving of even a single innocent is like saving the whole humanity.

The current acts of terror and violence have been associated with Islam and Muslims for political reasons. One can not at all excuse those undertaking these inhuman actions in any case. But one also had to see that what we are witnessing has more to do with outside factors than with the teachings and traditions of any religion for that matter. Historically the process of modernization has been stifled in the Muslim countries of the oil zone and also some other ones.

Formation of Israel, eviction of over a million Palestinians was the starting point. Interestingly the response from these Palestinians, the one in the form of terrorism, was not in the language of Islam. The overthrowing of Mossadeq, when he nationalized the oil wells in Iran(1953), harming the interests of US-UK oil companies put the brake on the process of modernization in the region.

Rulers of Saudi Arabia were constantly under the political umbrella of imperialists and it is here that the fanatic variety of Islam the Wahabi one, was nurtured. The US interests promoted the Sheikhdom and suppressed any inkling of modernization. At the same time, the Wahabi version of Islam backed up the feudal rulers to fulfill their personal ambitions of power and the lust of US for oil. With the Russian armies marching into Afghanistan in late seventies, the same Islam was made the base of training of Mujahidins to fight the Russian armies and financial and logistic support of US-Saudi-Pakistan is there for all to see. The political ambitions have been given the clever veneer of religion. Most of the phenomenon has internal and external factors, which created the whole. In case of the present so called Islamic terrorism, the external factors do dominate. It is good to look for the internal factors by Muslims. But what are they?

The fanatics on other side of the divide are happy that with the global propaganda around Islam as the culprit they can derive legitimacy for their own agenda, the way Hindutva is doing in India, the way Christian fundamentalism is coming up in US, the way US-UK axis has used it to attack these countries in rapid succession. Unless we can distinguish the boundaries of religion and the methods of politics, religion can always be dragged into the net of political goals.

The bombing on the Parliament has shaken us all to the core. This coming in the aftermath of WTC bombing is still more frightening. While words are not enough to condemn these heinous crimes by the terrorists, a new dimension has been added up in the tragic scenario, and that pertains to its association with Jihad, Islam and Muslims. On one hand the social common sense is being subtly doctored to believe that Islam as a religion gives rise to terror and Jihad, which is an integral part of Islam, means violence and aggression.

On the other hand the means to tackle terrorism have been defined, which essentially focus around tightening of security, intelligence, etc. A prescription to harden the Nation and society is being dished out as it is being said that we as a Nation are victims of terrorism as we have become a soft society and soft Nation. Also some talk is in the air to launch an aggression on the neighbouring country where the terrorist camps are located.

Myopia at its worst is on display. Can violence originate from any religion worth its spirituality? Does Jihad mean violence?

Is there terrorism because we are a soft society and Nation? These understandings have serious flaws, as they do not look beyond the nose of those promoting these ideas.

How is Islam related to terror, or for that matter how is any religion related to the cult of violence? Were the crusades undertaken by Christian kings to promote Christianity? Did Muslim kings undertake Jihad to promote Islam? Were the Dharmayudhas by Hindu kings undertaken to promote Hindu religion? By no stretch of imagination any war related violence could be attributed to these religions. It is the kings whose basic goal was to expand their kingdoms, who undertook these wars and misused the names of their religions to get more people involved in the same.

Timothy Mc Viehg, Oklahoma bomber was not serving Christianity, neither Dhanu was serving Hinduism when she acted as a live bomb killing Rajiv Gandhi and innocents around him, nor was Bhindranwale serving Sikhism when he promoted the cult of violence which led to murder of Indira Gandhi and then the butchery of thousands of Sikhs, nor was Osama bin-Laden serving Islam when he thanked Allah in the wake of the WTC tragedy, nor are the Kashmiri militants serving Islam when they maim and kill innocent Hindus and Muslims in the Valley of Kashmir.

Terrorism is the product of social and National discontent, which flows through the barrel of the gun or explodes with the bomb of terrorist when the democratic channels are not available for its expression for the victims of injustice. People belonging practically to all the religions under the sun have resorted to terror in the name of their religions. It is not that only one religion has the distinction for this misuse.

In Indian context the terrorism of Khalistanis could be contained when the dealing with the militants could be combined with winning over the hearts and minds of people and by making available the effective democratic options to the people at large. The present terrorism by the self proclaimed Jihadis is definitely a slightly different ball game. The role of Pakistan in this is very discernible. But here our myopic vision stops and fails to see the imperialist designs in promoting the terrorism and routing this through the conduit of Pakistan.

We are unable to see the deeper imperialist goals of control over oil resources, which has nurtured Talibans. Our policy makers are eager to jump to the softness thesis so that POTO or the worse forms of violations of civil liberties can be brought in with ease. So that they can get away with their other hidden agenda of creating a religious fascist state. It is surprising that our Govt. is prostrating in front of the very power, is touching the feet with reverence of the very imperialist power, which has promoted the cult of violence, the cult of Jihad to ensure its control over the oil resources by controlling the political power in the subcontinent.

Right since the formation of Israel and its being backed by US, the signals were around of its designs in the Middle East and then in the sub-continent.

Israel went into violate all the UN resolutions, attack Arab world repeatedly, to capture the Palestinian lands and to cause the loss of home and hearth of close to a million Palestinians.

In due course US started tightening its grip on the resources of the region. First it helped in the ouster of Mossadeq (Iran), who was planning to nationalize its oil wells and replacing that by a puppet Raza Shah Pehlavi regime to ensure the cheap flow of oil into its tanks. Later it went all out to promote the fanatic groups in the Afghanistan to fight the Russian occupation.

Since then the base for the fanatic camps was laid in the region. Pakistan as the handmaiden of US imperialism kept acting as the conduit to promote the US interests by all possible means. US to keep its hegemony in the region was playing different games. With Ayatullah Khomeini replacing the US stooge Raza Shah Pehlavi; US backed Iraq, in Iran-Iraq war for long years.

Later it turned its barrel against Iraq itself on the pretext of rescuing the Sheikh of Kuwait and his sovereignty. With the Russian occupation being pushed back, the fanatics, basically products of US training, started intruding into Kashmir, in the process worsening the Kashmir imbroglio, where due to weak democratic institutions the alienation of Kashmiri people acted as the base for the terrorist game and the green valley turned red with the bullets flowing from the barrels of militants and the Indian army.

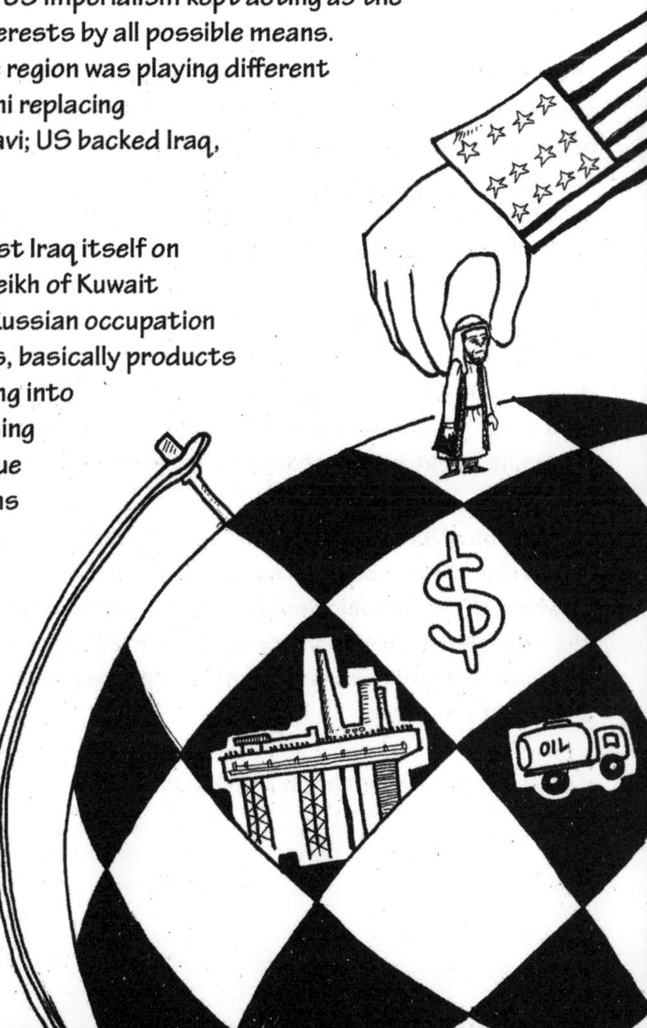

The dissatisfaction in the Arab world initially got manifested through the terrorist attacks on Jews. The terrorism here had two dimensions, one anti-Israel-US and later anti-Soviet occupation. US encouraged the latter through the conduit of ISI. Now after 9/11 the cycle has turned full circle giving further pretext to US to interfere more in the affairs of the region. The end of Socialist block has also marked the beginning of the demise of the role and power of UN, whatever it was worth.

With US acting as the supercop and superbullly rolled into one, the problems do not seem to have their respite. So contrary to US's own attitude vis a vis 9/11, a blind reprisal and aggression on Afghanistan, it is advising restraint to India on one hand and increasing its own grip in the region on the other.

No amount of hardness of Indian society and state, as if it is not violative of civil libertarian norms already, can solve the problem in the present set up where US hegemonic designs are on their naked march. While on one hand the intensification of military vigil and intelligence can act as a short term measure, the region cannot breathe in peace unless it is left to itself sans the US interference.

Removal of US hegemony in the region is a must for any possibility of peace.

The regional confederation of Middle East and South Asian countries on the line of European Commonwealth should not be a goal meant for dreams but an urgent necessity. Along with UN, the movement, which has suffered a serious set back is the Non-Aligned Movement. It's a tough task to restore and further strengthen NAM and to expand the SAARC into an Asian Commonwealth, but that seems to be the only base around which we can think of sidetracking the US designs in the area and bring and end to the symptom of terrorism in the region. In a way this symptom is secondary to the primary disease of Imperialism.

Terrorism is not a disease, it is a symptom of the underlying disease, the disease which manifested first in the form of Colonialism (projected as white man's burden) then went on to crushing the Nationalism in different countries, Vietnam, Chile, etc, in the name of defence of freedom and now is further continuing its agenda in the name of clash of civilizations, the economic lust of more advanced countries to control the resources of weaker countries and to create market for their goods in these countries.

The choice before us is either to buy the logic promoted by these powerful countries and focus on the superficial symptom of terrorism and to demonize one religion, or to have some vision and prepare to chart out a long-term goal of Asian Commonwealth.

Competitive Terrorism

One more act of blast took place on 10th Feb., 2007 in Nanded, city in the remote interiors of Maharashtra, in the wee hours of the morning. On the next day, the initial media reports did describe it as a blast. It took place in a biscuit shop, Amol biscuits.

It was a low key reporting in the media. In this blast one person, Pandurang Amilkanthwar, died instantly and another, Dyaneshwar Manikwar, sufferd 70% burns and succumbed to his injuries on the 6th day. In the initial statement, Manikwar said that it was an electric short-circuit. The next day he retracted his statement to say that he and Pandurang had deliberately put fire by using petrol to claim the insurance money as they were having financial problems.

Police and a section of media promptly accepted this version and stated that there was no political angle involved in the case, overlooking the fact that Pandurang was a Shiv Sena Pramukh, who was close to Bajrang Dal also. Just to recapitulate a year ago (April 6, 2006), in Nanded, in a blast , two Bajrang Dal workers were killed while making a bomb. The police explained it as a burst of crackers. But the impact of the blast was too strong and the police version stood exposed. The blast shattered the windows in the surrounding area of over a kilometer.

The house search revealed the powerful bomb, with a timer and remote control, after which the Inspector General of police conceded that it was a bomb blast and that those involved in the blast are the members of Bajrang Dal. Local papers reported that a diary has been found at the spot, which has the details of bomb making techniques and other relevant information. The local BJP MP stated that it was a minor incident. Meanwhile all the top leadership of RSS, VHP visited the hospital to see the injured and mourn the dead.

The police did arrest some fourteen people who were close associates of the ones who died. But they were all released, as the charges under which they were arrested related to minor offence only. Also the police/state pleader had no objections if the bail was granted to the arrested ones. The Bajrang Dal chief and the other activists of the Dal were left untouched despite the correlation of blasts with this RSS affiliation. Anti Terrorist Squad Inspector General K.P. Raghuvanshi stated that the explosives and the other weapons seized on the spot indicated that they were being trained in making bombs and operating firearms. They also started investigating the possible involvement of Bajrang Dal, an RSS affiliate in a blast outside a mosque in Parbhani, two years ago.

One recalls that there were series of episodes and blasts in Maharashtra in Parbhani, Purna, Jalna, Mumbai and Malegaon. The most disturbing of these were the train blast in Mumbai, July 11, 2006 and Malegaon on September 8, 2006. The timing of the blasts shows a clear pattern, barring in Mumbai, it was outside the mosques and in afternoons. In the aftermath of the Mumbai train blasts hundreds of Muslim youth were recklessly arrested in the Malvani area of Mumbai. In other places also many youth were put behind the bars on the slightest suspicion. This bias in police attitude was so blatant that in Malvani, the local people took the procession to the police station to get the innocent youth released.

In Malegaon blast also, which took on the day of Shab-e-Barat outside the Mosque near Bada Kabristan, police acted on the ground that Muslim groups are involved in the process. Here also the arrests were mostly of those who had minority identity. Some of those with previous SIMI connection were the easy targets. The local Muslim community was so disgusted with the attitude of the state and the police that it refused to accept the relief offered by the Chief Minister of the state under whose nose the biased attitude of police was clearly discernible. Interestingly in Malegaon police had been on high alert during the Ganapati festival, and dropped guards when it was Shab-e-Barat. The premise being, it was Muslims who created problems during Hindu festivals, else all is heavenly peace. The police had failed to take adequate precautions on a day prior to Shab-e-Barat. They also expressed their frustration by boycotting the meeting called by Minority Commission and the panel which went to study the situation in the city.

The brain mapping and Narco test of the Nanded blast accused of 2006, (http;//communalism.blogspot.com/search/label/maharashtra) revealed that Nanded was acting as the Bomb Nirmiti Kendra (Center for Making Bombs), guided and supported by the state level VHP and Bajrang Dal leaders. The plan was to make explosions in front of the mosques on Friday afternoons around 2 pm, when the attendance of the mosques is maximum. Himanshu Panse, the one who died while making a bomb is known to have stated that unless, Hindus do the blasts near mosques, it will be percieved as if Hindus were Hijras. The blasts are the only way to stop the attacks like the one in Varanasi and Delhi.

Coming on the heels of this Malegaon episode, the explanation given for the current 2007, Nanded incident was very puzzling. The Citizens Committee (http://www.sabrang.com/nanded/nanded.htm), which investigated the incident pointed out that the deceased changed his statement within hours.
In the current event, a scooter parked on the side of the road at some distance got burnt, the presence of nails and blades, gas cylinder in the room remaining unaffected and some food items not catching fire, indicated that there is a possibility of blasts. The committee amongst others comprised of the retired High Court Judge of Maharashtra, Justice Kolse Patil and noted social worker, Teesta Setalvad. The committee with the help of on sight inspections, interviews and opinions of forensic experts concludes that it was not a short circuit fire. The available evidence leads it to opine that it might have been an explosion caused due to an accident during the preparation of liquid bomb. It might have been due to combination of liquid inflammable substances. Surprisingly similar techniques have also been used in causing the blast in Samjhauta Express, in which most of those killed were poor Muslims.

One wonders what is happening to the investigations in such matters of serious concern. The contrast in the treatment of accused of two religious communities is glaringly obvious. We know the attitude and high handedness of the state and police authorities in dealing with Mumbai and Malegaon blasts, one has seen the 'promptness' of the authorities in apprehending anybody from the Muslim minority even on the slightest pretext and to keep such person in the custody on one ground or other.

There are too many gory tales about the lock up deaths and the type of treatment meted out to some of the accused. In the case of Nanded blasts, the one of 2006 and the one of 2007, despite the narco test report and brain mapping the inaction shown by the authorities concerned is totally baffling.

The new Police Commissioner of Mumbai, Dhananjay Jadhav, has stated that tackling terrorism will be on top of his priority list. What does he mean? Will he at least try to look at all the evidence in an impartial way to punish the guilty and protect the innocent? Will he break the shackles of prejudices binding the police force by dealing with the minorities? If that's what he means, it is a welcome sign for the state riddled with so many acts of terror. There he needs a turnaround in the policy of the state government and police officials who have been taking a blind partisan view and attitude in the investigation of the events like this.

The conclusion reached by the committee, more so in the wake of earlier similar blast in Nanded, and the efforts to present sop stories to cover up the incidents point to the deeper conspiracy hatched by groups equally insane and fanatic as the ones belonging to Al Qaeda are. What is surprising is that the so called secular government of Maharashtra which got elected on the secular ground, on the ground that it will implement the Srikrishna Commission report which it never did of course, has been very biased in its policies as reflected in the investigations done in the cases of Mumbai and Malegaon blasts. It has failed to connect the Nanded blasts of 2006 and has treated these incidents with jaundiced vision.

None of the functionaries of Bajrang Dal have been taken to task, and the parent organization of Bajrang Dal, RSS sits pretty. It's time Central Government intervenes and inquiry of all terror incidents in Maharashtra is handed over to CBI or preferably to the committee headed by a judge of impeccable credentials. Are Sonia Gandhi and Manmohan Singh listening?

APPENDIX-6

Civilization

CLASH OR ALLIANCE

During last two decades, the World has seen the rise of politics based on religious identity. Particularly after the 9/11 2001 WTC disaster there is a widespread feeling that Samuel Huntington's thesis, that after the end of cold war the current time is the one of Clash of Civilizations (Clash), is true. One has witnessed many a controversies where religion has been dragged into the murky world of politics. Osama bin Laden talked of Jihad and George Bush responded to the WTC attack by uttering that it is going to be Crusade for him.

He and his associate Blair both gave divine reasons for attack on Iraq. Multitude of controversies veered around Danish cartoons, Pope's statement about Islam, the banning of burqa in some Western countries, the rise of acts of terror in the name of Islam with the epithet coming that all terrorists are Muslims, has become popular in the social thinking at broad layers.

Superficially it is projected as if it is the clash between the Islamic culture and the Western civilization. Here in India also, attempts were made and are underway to project Islam as a religion of violence and Muslims being fanatics out to stick to the medieval social norms. The overall impact of the events and acceptance of this Clash thesis by Huntington has worsened the problem and is widening the intercommunity rifts.

As such the term clash of civilization was put forward by Bernard Lewis and later on converted into a thesis by Samuel Huntington, whose essay in a journal, Foreign Affairs 1993, became more popular after the 9/11 2001.

At the end of cold war Francis Fukuyama postulated 'End of History', which stood for "What we may be witnessing is not just the end of the Cold War, or the passing of a particular period of post-war history, but the end of history as such: that is, the end point of mankind's ideological evolution and the universalization of Western liberal democracy as the final form of human government." (quoted from "The End of History?", 1989) This was in response to the philosophy of Karl Marx, whose Historical Materialism propounded that the struggle between the classes is the cause of progress of society, leading to the classless society and end of History, i.e. beginning of classless, commune based society, communism.

In the backdrop of Fukuyama's 'End of History', Huntington postulated that while the age of ideology (Marxism, classless society) has ended with the collapse of Soviet system, the World has only reverted to the state of cultural conflicts. As per him the primary axis of conflict will be along cultural religious lines. The principal conflicts of global politics will occur between nations and groups of different civilizations.

The clash of civilization will dominate global politics and fault lines between civilizations are the battle lines of future. As per him, “It is my hypothesis that the fundamental source of conflict in this new World will not be primarily ideological or primarily economic. The great divisions among humankind and the dominating source of conflict, will be the cultural. Nation states will remain the most powerful actors in world affairs, but the principal conflicts of global politics will occur between Nations and groups of different civilizations. The clash of civilizations will dominate global politics. The fault lines between civilizations will be the battle lines of the future."

Many did approve of this thesis and the accompanying classification, whose main criterion is religion. This thesis did create an anxiety and confusion adding to the problems of the nations all around. It is in this context that Kofi Annan, Secretary General of UN launched an initiative co-sponsored by Prime Ministers of Spain and Turkey for an Alliance of Civilization in August 2005.

This initiative nominated a high level group cutting across different religions and nations to come up with an understanding of the world today and to recommend the measures to restore the amity of civilizations, cultures and people of the World. The report has been recently (mid Nov. 2006) submitted to the Secretary -General (http://www.unaoc.org/repository/report.htm)and it's a landmark in more ways than one.

It debunks the Clash thesis to bring our attention to the alliance between different cultures, nations and people at all the levels social, political and economic. It is not only in current times but since the times people started migrating and interacting that the alliance has been the undercurrent of the societal life. The report points out that Clash theory has distorted the terms of discourse on the real nature of predicament the world is facing. The history of relations between cultures is not only one of wars and confrontations; it is also based on centuries of constructive exchanges, cross fertilizations and peaceful co-existence. One is reminded here that India's ex-president, Dr. K.R.Narayanan, in response to the Clash thesis, said that civilizations don't clash, it is barbarisms which clash.

In Clash thesis, cultures and religions are identified with the religions of the kings and their wars are presented as clash between religions or civilizations.The Hate ideology spread by communal groups right here in South Asia also bases itself on the wars between Kings of different religions and these kings are presented as symbols of that religion. The whole aspect of cultural interaction is missing in this discourse. For example in India while the atrocities of Aurangzeb are the core of building the Hate ideology, the confluence articulated by Dara Shikoh as one can glean through his book Majma Ul Bahrain, India being a confluence of different cultures, is missing in this mindset. Similarly the rule of Muslim kings in the subcontinent is taken as the point for legitimization of Islamic nation.

The worst part of this Clash thesis is that by propagating that cultures are set on collision course, it helps in turning the negotiable disputes into seemingly intractable, identity based conflicts and this is what has taken control of popular imagination.

The report is based on the multipolar perspective and the UN Charter of Human rights. Significantly it points out that there is no hierarchy amongst cultures as each of them has contributed to the evolution of mankind. While the core problem remains poverty and deprivation of vast sections of mankind the rising trend of terrorism cannot be dealt with by seeing it as a mere law and order problem or having its roots in religion. On the contrary terrorism itself is a product of political circumstances, which need to be solved on urgent basis.

In societies if some groups are discriminated against violent repercussions come up and are perceived as libratory by a section of people while the same is seen as anti national by the state and other set of people. The durable solution to the causes of terrorism does not lie in attacking some countries or increasing the role of armed personnel in that area but in addressing the roots of resentment.

It traces the roots of current violent responses in the partition of Palestine and formation of Israel, and latter's occupation of part of Palestine and other Arab territories, which has come to be seen as a sort of colonialism by vast mass of people. While Jerusalem remains holy for Jews, Christians and Muslims, the support of Western powers to Israel's highhandedness is perceived as the collusion of West with the expansionism of Israel.

The committee is very clear on the point that no cause can justify the killing of civilians, non combatants. It does call for freedom of religions and takes a strong stand against desecration of holy places, irrespective of the majority minority religions. The report does recommend several measures in the arena of education, youth programs, community actions aimed to promote alliance, peaking it with the recommendation that a forum of alliance of civilization under the auspices of UN should be established and this should be promoted at all the levels national, societal and what have you.

The humane spirit of the report is visible all through. However the point is, in current times when the very authority of UN has been undermined by the powers that are arrogant, can we look forward to the era of Alliance and Amity so that the real problems gnawing the vast numbers of human kinds are properly addressed to, i.e. march in the direction of a better world, i.e. struggle for human rights. To put it in another way, is it possible to think positively, to think that 'Another World is possible', a World where Human rights of all of us are adhered to.

A. Social Movements - Tasks ahead

1. The communal and terrorist violence has been worsening over the years, more so from last two decades. The role of popular perceptions, the mass consciousness is very crucial in these acts of violence. The trivia, which comes in the form of spreading false hood about history and other things, like the nature of the other community etc. has gripped the social thinking. Every new episode of violence intensifies this social common sense, and one can say this doctored mass consciousness forms the base on which communal politics operates. In a way, this communal agenda has hegemonized the mindset of vast sections of society. Violating the harmony and syncretism every new episode of violence gives the confidence to the communal forces that they can operate from higher level and benefit in electoral ground also.

2. This hides behind itself the creeping communalization of society, through word of mouth, media and other social interventions of communalists. Also anti-minority sentiment gets intensified with every act committed by terrorists, with every act of communal violence. The erosion of objectivity of social and political institutions is going on at a fast pace.

3. The social movements for Human Rights while seriously concerned about the offensive of sectarian politics and terrorist violence are unable to find the suitable alternative ground for building a democratic plural platform.

4. Different parts of country show that communal forces have learnt faster, that the emotional issue (Ram Temple) and polarization (communal violence) are the basic mechanisms, which bring them to power.

In consequence the present strategy for peace has to take into consideration these problems.

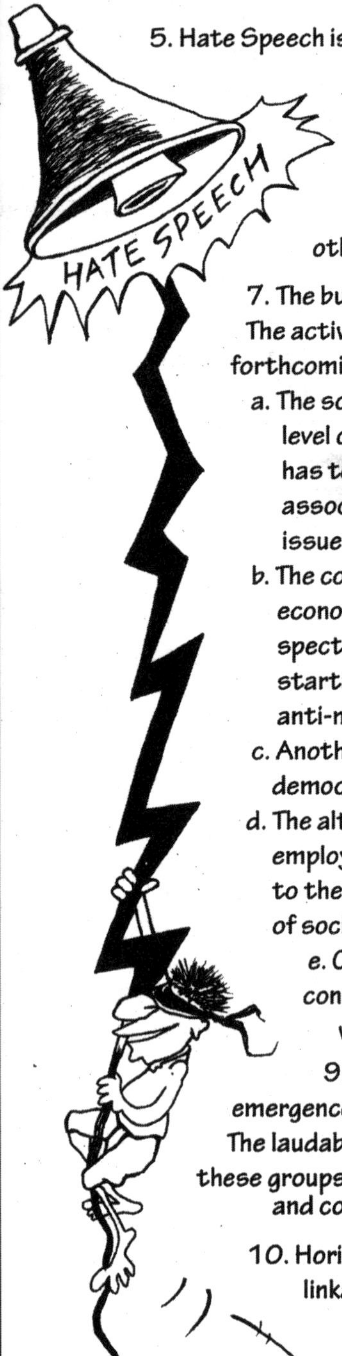

5. Hate Speech is dominating the social scene. The identity politics resorted by communalists is trying to overshadow the politics for democratic values.

6. The response of those trying to save the democracy and Indian constitution has to be supplementary to each other and coordinated, if possible.

7. The building up of democratic platform has to be many layered. The activists of social movements are the Base of the forthcoming struggle.

a. The social movement's aspirations have to be coalesced at the level of programs. The fragmentation of the progressive forces has to be addressed and to begin with, a loose programmatic association of different groups has to be evolved around the issues of downtrodden.

b. The core problems, which need urgent attention, relate to economic rights, social equality and gender justice. In the spectrum of issues to be taken up there can be a long list starting from employment rights to anti-Dalit, anti-women, anti-minority atrocities.

c. Another layer of the struggle is the one related to civil and democratic liberties.

d. The alternative schemes for most of these sections, employment, protection, education, work etc. has to be linked to the communitarian and social life of the weaker sections of society.

e. Countering communal politics at the level of social consciousness has to be linked to efforts to promote secular values and education.

9. The positive fallout of last few years is the emergence of forums to work on these issues. The laudable work being done by these groups needs sustenance and coordination.

10. Horizontal, issue based, linkage of the groups working on these issues will be mutually strengthening.

B. Need for Education related to Secular Values

1. Rising communal and terrorist violence has more than ever before brought to our notice the communalization of society.

   This process begins with doctoring of the minds of people in general and later gets transformed into hate for the other and forms the basis of various communal actions, the most glaring of which is communal violence.

   It also brings along a silent sanction to the communal policies being pursued at different levels.

2. Communal forces have been working on doctoring of the minds from last many decades. Communalization process is assisted by:

   a. The communal slant of school books, which gets worsened with violence, and communal curricula.

   b. The media has a strong role in the process, especially large section of the language press and English media to some extent spread it in a strong way. There are sections of media which deliberately spread divisiveness, and other which are influenced by it.

   c. Most of the cultural space has also been hegemonized by the communal ideology.

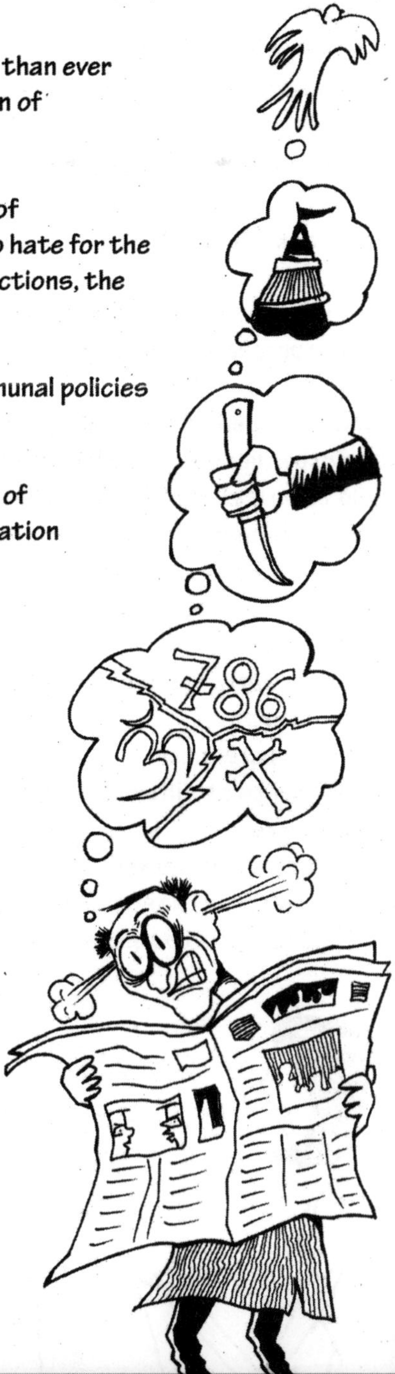

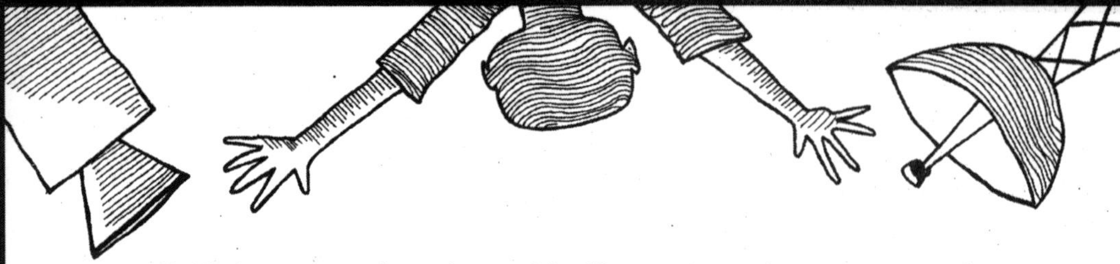

3. We have to work against odds. The myths and stereotypes about minorities abound and form the base for the communal consciousness.

4. The formation of these ideas begins from early age and keeps getting stronger.

5. The task of education has to take into consideration that:

a. Discussions alone cannot transform the societal consciousness.
b. The process of social education in the values of harmony has to be:

A multi-pronged effort in which intervention in media, cultural programs and direct interactive discussions with different layers of society are the integral components, needs to be undertaken. Also these efforts have to have a reference point of the social movements for social, economic and gender justice.

6. In order of importance and logistics the following groups have to be approached:

a. Social activists/Government institutions already involved with promotion of harmony.
b. Media personnel
c. Students at different levels
d. Teachers
e. The groups of workers, dalits, women and adivasis through their associations and through Basti associations.
f. If possible the liberal sections of society through different clubs.

7. Some groups can specialize in cultural and media intervention. The cultural activities include street theatre, song groups, local cultural expressions (Powadas, Quawallis etc.)

Street theatre seems to be most feasible and effective media of expressions. Showing of films has a great impact.

8. Discussion and Lectures- the workshops of activists, students and teachers can be one major conduit.

The Basti conventions by political activists are another major ones. Teachers can be approached through their associations, students through NSS/Nehru Yuva Kendra and other forums of the colleges.

9. The topics to be covered in sequential order can be as follows:

a. Myths about medieval history, temple destructions, forcible conversions, alliances of kings, syncretic traditions, saints and sufis, culture and religion.

b. Religion and Human society, Aspects of Religions, types of religions- Adivasi, regional, Prophet based. Evolution of the concept of God, religious communities in India.

c. Freedom Struggle- Secularization process, transformation of social relations of caste and gender, British in India, Formation and goals of Indian National Congress, Rise of Communal politics-its goals, Muslim League,Hindu Mahasabha

d. Partition tragedy and Kashmir Problem

e. Communal Violence and politics in Post independence India, decade of 80s, Meenakshipuram, Shah Bano, Ghettoisation of Minorities, Uniform civil code

f. Stereotypes of minorities-four wives: Twenty Children, Loyalty to Pakistan, conservatism

g. Terrorism, Imperialism and Islam

h. Communalism -Genesis, growth, agenda

i. Struggle for secular society,

10. The discussions need to be backed up by

a. Projects-meet the people from minority community, interact observe Paper cuttings about crime, communal violence, being part of riot investigation team, mohalla committees

b. Sharing of resources-books, cassettes, bibliography

c. Libraries with above materials

d. Formation of work groups for different activities, innovative community functions

C. Need for Training Peace Activists: Training for trainers:

1. Many groups are seriously conducting the programs (e.g. CSSS and ANHAD in particular) on Peace and conflict resolution, political training in the face of threat of rising fascism. These programs range from 2to 7 days workshops on Peace and conflict resolution. These cover most of the topics mentioned above. In addition many a groups are having lecture programs opposing communalism. The message is reaching out to a section of people but it is not adequate in the face of the challenge of communal forces.

2. There is a need to broaden this work in a form, which can reach to broad layers of society. For this, from amongst those who have attended different types of workshops and are willing and have time to work for these issues need to be encouraged and trained further. This training/interaction will involve:

   a. They going through a set of books, seeing films and magazines on these themes.

   b. With this preparation of around six months they assemble and we have group discussions, they discuss each of our usual topics and the moderator just assists them to come to proper understanding.

   c. They are given a set of social situations related to communalism-conflict and politics and discuss to overcome that. We select a set of 30 activists each time, and make them discuss in smaller groups, the themes about communalism and concrete problems, and how do we respond to them. The discussion is moderated by resource persons, who sum up the discussion at the end.

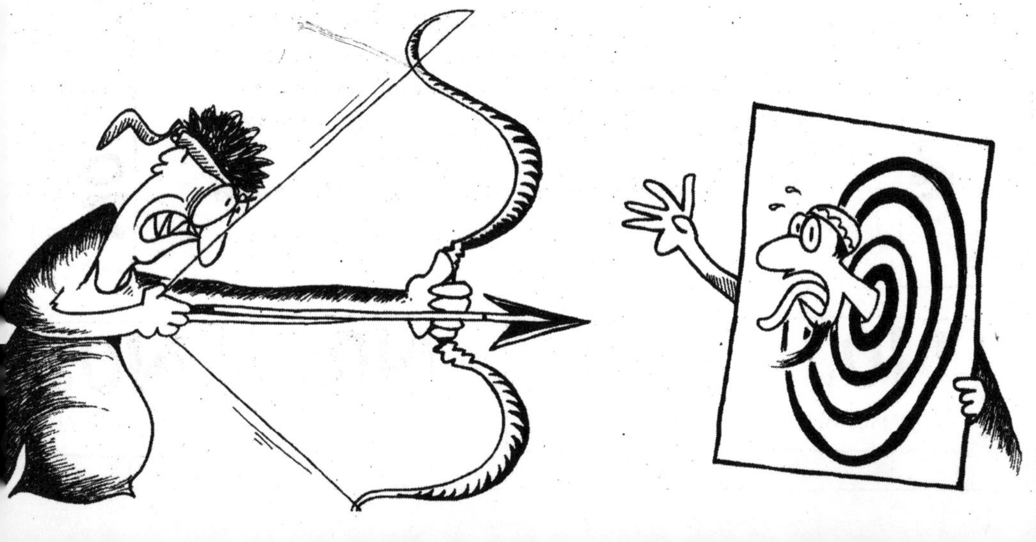

3. These activists, peace workers for secular democracy work in their areas, adding on to the facilities of existing community centers to incorporate the material on communal harmony or setting up resource centers, assisted by or in conjunction with the existing groups.

4. These peace workers can do multiple tasks:

   a. Managing community resource center

   b. Ensuring the screening of films in small groups and then conducting discussions around that.

   c. Organizing intercommunity programs, festivals or national events

   d. Organize programs for the activists/cultural workers visiting the area

   e. Interacting with school colleges for showing exhibitions/guiding the viewing of educational videos like Raah Aman Ki, In Defence of Our freedom, Final Solution, Ham Sab Ek hain etc. Planning quiz competitions and other competitions around the themes of national integration -communal harmony

   f. Various other programs suitable for the community

D. Community Centers: Resource Center: Peace Center

We need to work at multiple levels. Apart from the awareness programs we have to supplement cultural expressions and mechanisms in our work in our existing centers for community/offices we can add the material and program for these things.

The core point is to have gadgets for showing films to small groups, (TV/Computer + DVD player). Either existing centers can be boosted or new one's planned along these lines. The peace worker in charge assist the process of seeing films/ discussions/ does story telling for children/organizes intercommunity festivals and national day e.g. Gandhi, Bhagat Singh, and Ambedkar.

This community center also ensures that peace prevails through intercommunity interaction and propagation of proactive humane values and concept of rights of weak in simple and effective methods, in a language which people understand.

We can draw out a community work calendar, which can be modified according to local needs. We need to begin the translation/dubbing and modification of existing audio, visual and print material. These can be newly set up centers or these may be add on to the existing community centers.

E. Reading material and Material for Resource Centers

1. The local and state level resource centers should have facilities for showing films on computers or TV/DVD players.

2. The list of books can be picked up from the book, Striving for Secular Democracy (Vikas Adhyayan Kendra).
   To begin with simple books like:

   a. Asghar Ali Engineer: Medieval History, Communalism in India, Islam in 21st Century
   b. Basu, Datta Sarkar et al, Khaki Shorts Saffron Flag
   c. Bipan Chandra: Communalism -a Primer
   d. VAK: Lessons of Gujarat
   e. Ram Puniyani, Communalism: What is false What is True, Communalism: Illustrated Primer, Communalism: Facts versus myths, Terrorism: Facts versus Myths

3. Periodicals

A. Asghar Ali Engineer: Secular Perspective
B. Javed Anand, Teesta Setalvad: Communalism Combat
C. L.S. Hardenia: Secular, Socialist Bharat
D. Amir Ali Ajani: Navnirman

4. Films

a. Feature Films: Garam hava, Padosi,
Mr.& Mrs. Aiyer, Mammo, Nassem, Zakhm, Siskiyan, Black and White, Perzania, Khuda ke Liye, Zakhm, Dhokha, Firaq

b. Documentaries:

I : Anand Patwardhan: Ram Ke Naam, Father Son and Holy War, War and Peace

II: Vineet Tiwari: Jinhe Hind Par Naaz hai

III: Suma Jossan: Bombay's Blood Yatra, Ayodhya se Varanasi tak

IV: Madhushree Datta: I live in Behrampada

V: Rakesh Sharma: Final Solution

VI: Waqar Khan: Hum Sab Ek hain

VII: Subhradeep Chakrborty: Godhra Tak, Sohabuddin

VIII: Sharad Sharma: Chitti Hatia

c. Educational

CSSS; Raah Aman Ki

Anhad: In Defence of our Dreams

5. Song Cassettes

I Charul Bharvada, Vinay Mahajan: Insaan hain Ham

II Dharmendra

III Anhad

Poster Series

I: Anhad In Defence of Democracy

II: Ram Puniyani: Terrorism: Perceptions and Reality

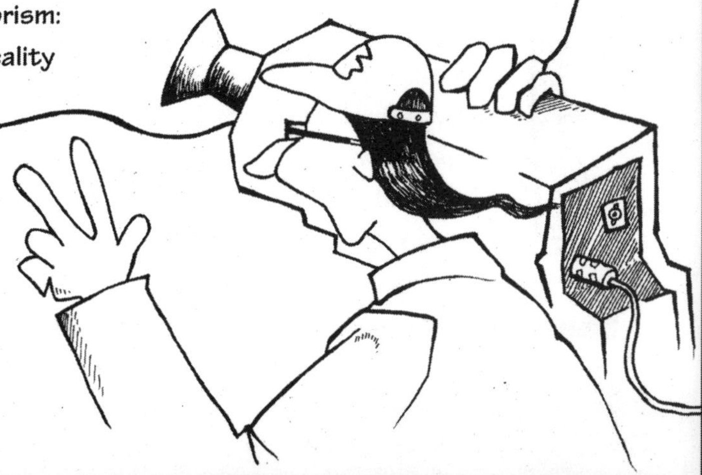

PEACE WORKER

These peace activists see this as an extension of their present work, addition to their present work, and we should see that a coordination/support structure is built up at state/national level to ensure that it goes on.

They take up local activities as per the local situation, the aim being promotion of intercommunity relations, countering the communal onslaught in the form of violence and political steps damaging secular ethos

F. 1 - Community Resource Centers: Programs

There is a need for social intervention at the level of awareness programs, cultural interaction and bridging the community divides. There are many community centers which are focusing on some

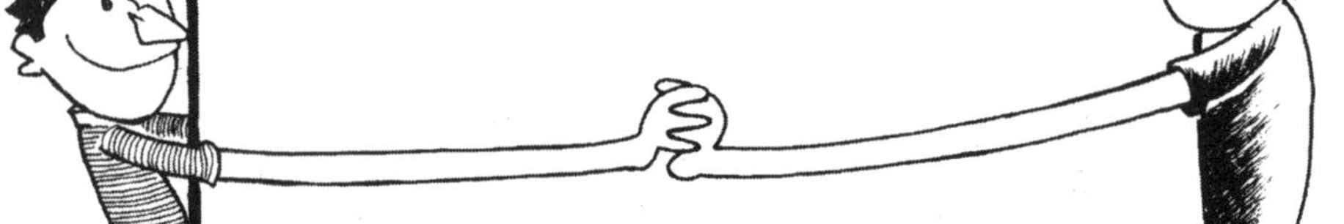

or the other community issue like education and health. These centers can be encouraged to keep material, films, posters, magazines, books on communal amity. The peace workers and community resource centers work in tandem, peace workers either set up or adopt the existing community centers and add the material related to National intégration/communal amity.

The peace worker, depending on her time organizes the film screenings for small groups, and undertakes discussions around those. Similarly posters and Powerpoint Presentations should be prepared, which the peace workers can use to communicate their ideas. Similarly more people can associate with the center and activities like film watching can be led by them.

These centers can also act as nidus for intercommunity programs, the programs around social aspects of religious festivals, around celebration of national festivals and the anniversaries of Gandhi, Ambedkar, Bhagat Singh etc. The same center can organize group discussions with the peace worker or those activists visiting that area.

We can, over a period of time see that the participants of PCRs get associated with this work in their areas. Some programs can also be evolved around the needs of children having vacations, like painting, drawing competitions. Summer training lectures for senior students and the community members.

Initiating a campaign against communalism using Grassroots Comics

So far, comics had been considered only as story books for children's reading but Grassroots Comics has presented comics as a powerful medium for common man's reading and expression. People did not only create comics on their own stories but has also started converting all their issues into comics form.

Since the beginning, Grassroots have been prepared in workshops and so comics have also been thought by some to be limited to the four walls of workshop hall. But the application and use of comics is not restricted to the workshop halls only; when these comics are photocopied and distributed among people, it leads to debate on the issue focused and here lies the important role of the comics.

Now, World Comics India have plenty of examples where comics have emerged out of the workshop hall and taken the guise of a campaign or people's movement. Be it the " Rajasthan's Girl Child Education Rights Campaign" or the "Goenkar Changemaker's Campaign" or "Chadi Ke Laagal Hathkadi Campaign" against corporal punishment in Uttar Pradesh, the power of comics is evident.

Grassroots Comics

Grassroots comics are not prepared by artists but by socially aware people themselves, based on their own understanding. These are also instrumental in initiating debates on such issues. Besides, preparing comics is quite easy and does not require heavy duty technical expertise of any kind. All you need is paper, pen and photocopy.

These comics are prepared for distribution at the local level, which is the main factor that distinguishes it from other campaign materials. After photocopying, these comics are pasted at common places where people would leisurely sit schools, bus-stops, shops, offices, notice boards and even electricity poles. Most of the times, readers are aware about the organization that has distributed these comics.

Connection is the most important point here. The readers and the people who have prepared this medium of information, practically, are not very different from each other. Common people of the society who feel strongly about any issues prepare their campaign materials themselves instead of getting them prepared by an artist from the capital or abroad.

One of the most important things for people is that when wall-poster comics are prepared on the view of the local people and organizations concerning an issue and are pasted on walls, not only do they understand the message conveyed but it also encourages debates among people.

Campaign against Communalism?

Running campaigns by using comics as a medium is a new concept. Generally, peoples' participation is the biggest challenge faced by campaigns that are run by using other media. Usually the materials used in a campaign are prepared by professionals with the help of good artists based in metro cities. In such a case, there are fewer chances that the materials will prove true and useful to the social and psychological set up of the people.

These difficulties are further accentuated by language and local environment. As such, these problems can be solved if the campaign materials are prepared by local people themselves. Besides, the participation of the family, friends and colleagues of the people who prepare these materials in the campaign is ensured.

Grassroots comics facilitate the local people to bring their own issues and experiences by presenting them in the form of a story. Once the people understand the technique of comic making then they can prepare comics on any given issue in no time. The power of sharing their view among people fills them with new enthusiasm.

Comics Workshop

These comics can play a crucial role in the campaign against communalism. A group of 20-25 participants have to be selected for this workshop. All of these participants will be key links in the campaign that would consequently lead to campaign as well.

Trainer's workshop

On the last two days of the five days workshop, the participants would be trained to train others. (Check Trainer's Manual and/or book Grassroots Comics, page No. 141). Now these new trainers would conduct similar comics workshops in their own area.

Exhibition and distribution

Exhibition is the best way to take the issues raised in the campaign among the people. As distinguished from an art-gallery exhibition, this is put up in a tent on the roadside and is open to the common people. This can be done by putting up a tent measuring 12 x 15 on the main street of any small area or city. All the campaign materials can be pasted on attractive colourful chart papers and displayed in the exhibition. Any passerby would get attracted to the exhibition and would want to take back some poster or booklet with him. This is an exciting experience to see how people express their eagerness to join the campaign themselves. A register could also be kept to note down their suggestions. This exhibition can be put up or removed within few minutes of time.

For details check World Comics India website www.worldcomicsindia.com
To download basic manual, trainers manual and campaign manual, use following link http://www.worldcomicsindia.com/youcanuse.html